When
Bad
Things
Happen to
Good
Crocheters

The Taunton Press

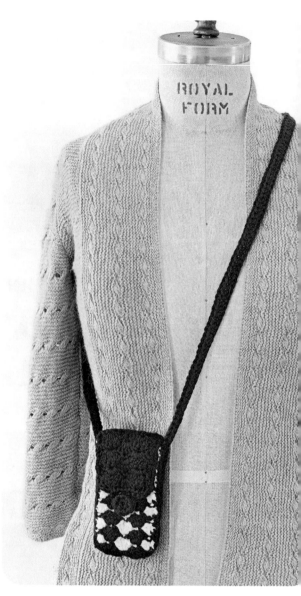

When
Bad
Things
Happen to
Good
Crocheters

SURVIVAL GUIDE *for*
EVERY CROCHETING
EMERGENCY

Beth Wolfensberger Singer

The Taunton Press

For Pearl and Wanda and Spike, my creative
dream team of problem solvers.

The Taunton Press, Inc., 63 South Main Street, PO Box 5506, Newtown, CT 06470-5506
e-mail: tp@taunton.com

Editors: Ashley Little, Shawna Mullen, Tim Stobierski
Copy editor: Betty Christiansen
Indexer: Cathy Goddard
Original cover design: Alison Wilkes
Cover illustrator: Peter Horjus
Original interior design: First edition design by 3+ Co.; revised and updated edition design
    by Rita Sowins/Sowins Design
Interior illustrator: Christine Erikson
Photographer: Scott Phillips except for pp. ii, 93, 96, 100, 106, 111, 114 by Alexandra Grablewski

The following names/manufacturers appearing in *When Bad Things Happen to Good Crocheters* are
trademarks: Barbie®, Bernat® Sheep(ish)™, Bernat® Softee®, Caron® Simply Soft®, Cotton-Ease®,
iPhone®, Lion Brand®, Loops & Threads® Impeccable™, Martha Stewart Crafts™, Red Heart® Soft®,
Rockettes®, Wool-Ease® Thick & Quick®

Library of Congress Cataloging-in-Publication Data

Names: Singer, Beth Wolfensberger, author.
Title: When bad things happen to good crocheters : survival guide for every
   crocheting emergency / Beth Wolfensberger Singer.
Description: Newtown, CT : Taunton Press, Inc., [2016] | Includes index.
Identifiers: LCCN 2016016796 | ISBN 9781627103947
Subjects: LCSH: Crocheting--Miscellanea. | Crocheting--Patterns.
Classification: LCC TT820 .S52763 2016 | DDC 746.43/4--dc23
LC record available at https://lccn.loc.gov/2016016796

Printed in the United States of America
10 9 8 7 6 5 4 3 2 1

Acknowledgments

Big fat thanks to my editors: Shawna Mullen, Timothy Stobierski, Carolyn Mandarano, and Ashley Little. You made this whole shebang fun. Also to my agent Colleen Mohyde, who believed in my designs, then hooked me up (get it?) with The Taunton Press over a beautiful cup of hot chocolate.

Additional gratitude to Astrid Gallet, for yarn and a pep talk, to fabulous photographers Scott Phillips and Alexandra Grablewski, and to all my Facebook friends for getting psyched about crochet with me even if it wasn't your thing.

Deepest thank yous to my amazing Noah and Niles, and especially David, for enabling me to focus on projects I love, and for tolerating yarn bits in every room. Last, special appreciation to Phoebe, who confidently models my most eccentric creations. This book exists to show avid readers like my girl how to crochet with minimal angst.

Contents

Introduction

Ack. Eeek! Oh, dang. What in the world? Seriously?

The above words, I've come to believe, are technical terms used now and then by crocheters at all levels of expertise—loosely speaking, that is. You don't see these terms in patterns. You never come to the place in the instructions where it says, "Ch 3, turn, notice funky bump. Increase doubt. Grumble across rest of row."

These things happen, though. They just do, darn it. And in the grand scheme of things, it's not a disaster, not really. Not like your house catching fire.

But it sure can feel like something's aflame when crochet trials descend. You hit a roadblock, some mystifying hiccup, however small, and it saps your precious crafting moments and your motivation. Especially if you look forward to your crochet time all day, and finally are plunked in your coziest chair with exciting new yarn in hand, and don't want to unfold yourself to fetch phone or computer to search for an expert who can address a problem that is kind of like yours (only not exactly), in a way you almost understand (but not fully).

That's where this book comes in. It's written precisely for that moment when you're in a jam and need guidance with 9-1-1 speed. Accidentally just snip a stitch clean in half? Go ahead: Curse like a sailor. Then take a deep breath and consult pp. 78–79 for reliable first aid. Wondering what that hole is, right where a hole was definitely never invited? Or why your row suddenly looks shorter than its predecessors? Chapter 3 is an excellent diagnostician, and possibly your new best friend. Cross-eyed over some crochet pattern abbreviation? Been there, done that, and then some, which is why we buffed and polished our second chapter to within an inch of its life. Behold: all the crochet abbreviations in plain Earth-person language. With vowels, even!

Having suffered frustration with other guidebooks, we've worked hard to make this one both comprehensive and a snap to skim, with clear headings that will escort you to the swiftest possible relief when you're in a pinch. And because many minds are better than one, we've gathered the best crochet disaster-prevention advice from a crew of accomplished, witty, and knowledgeable crochet stars. You'll find these experts piping up throughout the pages like reassuring yarn buddies, offering their favorite grief-saving tips and funny project stories. A crafter, after all, needs laughter.

The book opens with "Emergency Prevention 101," an easy-to-understand collection of strategies for bagging possible snags before they even happen. This chapter will help you corral everything you need in the way of tools, pick a project and yarn that minimize frustration, and get in a positive frame of mind. Chapter 2, "The Alien Language of Crochet Patterns," will decode those abbreviations fast, with clear illustrations to help, plus info on altering patterns for different sizes and gauges. Chapter 3 is the luscious main course: All the best recipes for dealing with assorted crochet emergencies, plus tragedy avoidance steps for the trickier stuff, along with pointers on drape and style, are here. Chapter 4, "Finishing Fiascos and How to Dodge Them," helps you wrap up that project with expert ease. No more adding to your hidden gallery of unfinished projects; we show how to finish strong. Rounding out the advice is Chapter 5, "Are You a Good Glitch or a Bad Glitch?" It speaks to which mistakes can be fudged. Or left in place. Or morphed into something wonderful.

Something wonderful, by the way, is possible, even in the most troubled crochet crises. Crochet mistakes, vexing as they may be, are always erasable, because you can rip out your work and start anew. Voilà: clean slate. That's why you'll notice such a lighthearted tone in these pages. We see the worst, we forgive, we chuckle, and we feel grateful for the learning. I've been crocheting like a fiend for 35 years, and I can't tell you how many times I've seen it happen: A big boo-boo magically becomes a lesson, leading to a new shaping technique or a realization that helps me unexpectedly.

Lastly, here's a promise. The pages you hold in hand contain decidedly good things you can make happen for sure: six delicious crochet patterns, from the perfect-gift chokers (with variations!), to a hip new spin on granny squares and a chunky scarf to sigh for.

It is truly my wish, and the wish of this book's talented contributors, that *When Bad Things Happen to Good Crocheters* becomes your instant treasured safety net, helping you soar without fear. And laugh. We hope you laugh, too.

Your Captain Hook,
Beth Wolfensberger Singer

 ## Crochet's Rough Birth?

Historians say there is scarce evidence anyone crocheted before the 1800s. But who asked a historian to chime in here, anyway? To our mind, the origin of crochet goes much further back and is obvious. It sprang from someone making a mistake. Perhaps some caveperson stumbled over the foot of her friend Gaaak near a woolly mammoth and unintentionally did the first chain stitches in mammoth hair while defending her life with a bent stick (then laughed about it for years as she hooked everyone cave-scarves). Or a medieval couple in an ugly divorce each got half of a set of knitting needles, and flailed around with them in anger until one discovered crochet and the other began hooking rugs. They lived happily separately ever after, among beautiful textiles.

Okay, dubious, dubious. But despite its outdated image as a staid pastime, crochet is a supremely playful activity, one almost certainly invented by someone open to messing up while experimenting with fiber. So when you're in a crochet bind, relax. Remember: Mistakes are how the whole thing started. Besides, you have this book. We'll get you back on track.

Emergency Prevention 101

We've seen them. Those cool crochet chicks who look like they could probably drive a sports car and hook up a scarf at the same time, all while telling jokes and listening attentively. It would be easy to resent such élan, but instead let's simply spill the secret behind it: basic preparation. Seriously, the crafters who make it look easy and fun aren't more yarntastically gifted than you. They're just prepared.

That's what this little chapter is all about and . . . Hey! You're tempted to skip these pages and go straight to the yummy patterns, aren't you? But give the following three safety tips a chance. They'll exempt you from a lot of groaning down the line.

Safety Tip #1: Stock That Bag, Soldier

Your crochet bag is your emergency supplies kit. In addition to the yarn and instructions you need for whatever your current project is, this mama should have everything within easy reach to get you out of common jams and back into your crafting flow. So clean out your favorite tote right now and toss these in:

- **This book.** But maybe in a few minutes, since you're currently reading it.

- **Scissors:** Doesn't matter what kind—all they're going to cut is yarn, but they can never leave the bag unless you are using them, and then they report right back, no exceptions (many experienced crafters would love a dollar for every minute of our lives we've spent tracking escaped scissors). Here's a lifesaving tip: Knot one end of a length of pretty ribbon around the handle of your scissors and the other end around a handle of the bag. Now you can always yank your snippers to the surface, and no one in your household can steal them from your bag without some effort.

- **Crochet hooks:** Do you have a favorite crochet hook yet? I do. When I can't find it, I'm beside myself, because it belonged to my talented Granny Pearl and probably still has her good vibes on it. It's hard to exaggerate the importance of identifying your One True Hook, but no matter which one it is, you'll also need an assortment of sizes for various parts of projects. Fortunately, it's cheap and easy to buy a whole set of crochet hooks, in sizes F (3.75 mm), G (4 mm), H (5 mm), I (5.5 mm), J (6 mm), and K (6.5 mm), and have those on hand at all times. Be extra vigilant about keeping these hooks in some kind of container you can grab easily when you fish around between all the yarn balls in your crochet bag. A sturdy plastic pencil case

works great, as does any kind of zippered pouch. Choose something that closes firmly, please, and you should always take the extra second to make sure it's totally closed.

- **A tapestry needle or two:** These are necessary for weaving in ends on finished pieces, sewing on details, and sewing pieces together. What they aren't necessary for is stabbing you under the fingernail when you reach into your bag. Or stabbing a loved one in the butt if you leave the needle on the couch while working. Be extra militant about your tapestry needle storage. Find a good, storage home for them. (Hint: An unsuspecting loved one's butt does not count as a good storage home.) I use a small plastic lidded container, and I often store the needle with a length of yarn still in the eye, so the needle is easier to spot. Then I always return them there, without fail. It doesn't matter whether your needle is plastic or metal, by the way. And the size of the needle doesn't really matter, either, though around a 16 or 18 is good. You want a needle whose eye is big enough to thread yarn through, basically.

- **Safety pins and some straight pins, too:** Useful for attaching notes to works in progress and for pinning finished pieces together.

- **A tape measure:** Because you'll be required to measure things now and then even if you would personally rather clean a toilet. Sorry.

- **Paper and something to write with:** You'll occasionally want to do some math or sketches and write yourself some notes. A notebook that really closes is the best choice here so the pages don't get all bent in the bag. Or you can put the notepad and/or sticky notes into their own plastic storage bag to prevent mangling.

- **Stitch markers:** Buy whatever kind you like or skip this for now, as stitch markers can be made from paper clips, safety pins, or even scraps of yarn. If you have real ones, store

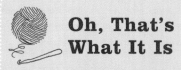

Oh, That's What It Is

If you see a hook that looks like the love child of a knitting needle and a crochet hook (hook on one end, stopper on other, long shank in between), you are probably looking at a Tunisian crochet hook, also known as an Afghan crochet hook, which, sorry, is kind of confusing given that *Afghan* is not only a synonym for *Tunisian* in this case, but also the name of those crocheted blankets made of granny squares. We'll cover how to do the basic Tunisian/Afghan thing on pp. 87–88. Like the hook, this type of crocheting seems to be a hybrid; it looks kind of like knitting, kind of like crochet. And hey, it turns out it's also called Scottish knitting. The crochet terminology people, whoever they are, obviously aren't that decisive.

- **A gauge measurer/hook sizer:** This isn't absolutely necessary but is a nice tool, because it helps you with measuring gauge (which you could do with your tape measure) and sizing your hooks (which are usually marked, but sometimes are hard to read). You'll notice they tend to work for knitting needles and knitting gauges also.

- **Adhesive bandages and granola bars (or another healthy snack):** Obviously not mandatory. But it's nice to be prepared for a paper cut or low-energy break, especially if they happen simultaneously.

- **One piece of delicious reading material (besides this book):** Why? Well, really and truly, sometimes the best thing you can do when you get frustrated with a project is give your mind a short break from it.

- **Oh yeah, and your yarn:** Chances are you'll end up with at least 10 balls of yarn of various sorts and sizes trying to intermingle in your crochet bag. It's cute of them to want to bond, but untangling is a waste of your time. So put each ball in its own zip-top bag, opened just enough, during a crochet session, to let the yarn end come out when you want it to (some like to seal the zip-top part of the bag and cut just a small hole in a corner for the yarn to thread out). The outside of each little bag is a good place to jot down where you bought the yarn. The yarn's label stays in this bag, too.

them either in the closed container with your tapestry needles or in their own little home of some kind; otherwise, guaranteed, they will crawl to the bottom of the bag and not feel worth scraping up. **Important:** Knitting stitch markers are often circular with no break in them, and so cannot be used as crochet stitch markers. Just read the packages carefully when buying.

Safety Tip #2: Mind Your Wand

It's kind of impossible to exaggerate the importance of finding the crochet hook that feels right to you. Okay, it's not *impossible* to exaggerate it. If someone said the hook would

A Connoisseur's Tour of the Hook

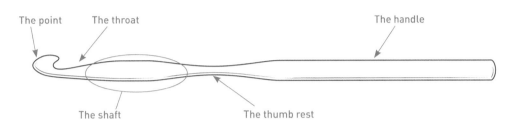

The point   The throat   The handle

The shaft   The thumb rest

- The point can be more or less rounded or pointy.

- The throat can be curved or more abruptly sliced.

- The shaft is where stitches are formed, so the thickness of it determines the size of the stitch.

- The thumb rest is a flattened area and very well named. On smaller hooks, it is hardly noticeable.

- The handle just hangs out, providing balance. But some handle shapes may appeal to you more than others.

save your life during an earthquake . . . yeah, don't trust that person. But to many crocheters, project happiness is largely dependent on the feel of what's going on in their hands. A good half of that is yarn, and the other half? It's all hook, baby.

Crochet hooks come in many confusing sizes and are made from various materials, including steel, aluminum, plastic, wood, and bamboo. Some have added gripping handles, some have a heft to them, and some are light. Some are beautifully carved from wood. Others have curved handles for ergonomic balance, or sweet little covers for the hook part.

Fortunately, most hooks are inexpensive, so experimenting to find which one suits you won't break the bank. For the fancier kinds, see if you can get permission to try them out gratis at your friendly local yarn shop.

You may notice that the material the hook is made from affects the feel of crocheting dramatically. Yarn slides quickly along a metal hook, which is a bonus for an experienced crocheter who wants to go fast, but it may be a tad unnerving to someone just starting off (or maybe not—again, you've gotta try it). A wooden crochet hook looks so colonial and natural and is never all chilled-out temperature-wise like a metal hook, but if you sit on the thinner ones the wrong way, you'll be looking at two broken pieces where you once had a useful tool. Also, yarn can snag on a wooden hook over time, and a wooden hook can slow down someone with faster fingers.

There are plastic hooks, especially in the larger sizes because they are lighter that way, but look at them carefully before buying, as some are not that well made and can have little seam edges where yarn can snag, which is basically a prescription for throwing the hook across the room in frustration.

Think of hook-searching as play. Try a bunch of chain stitches or single crochet rows using whatever yarns you have on hand in combination with whatever hooks you can locate/purchase cheaply/borrow from friends or shops. Things to consider are how the head (hook end) is shaped—some are more rounded and some have more of an abrupt cut under the hook—and also how the rest of it feels in your hand. You will discover the one that suits you better, and it's okay to change your mind about that later. Simply be aware that this is an important part of the crafty happiness equation, and that what works for your crochet mentor will not necessarily be your fave.

WHAT'S THE DEALIO WITH HOOK SIZES?

Hook sizing is basically quite messed up. That's the story. Maybe in the future it won't be, but right now: big time. There are letter names for hooks, and also number names for the same hooks. There are different numbering systems for the smaller hooks, which are made of steel and are also called thread hooks, and there is a whole different system of numbering hooks from the U.K., which is the reverse of the U.S. system, *naturally*. Even though A is clearly the very first letter of the alphabet, as far as I can tell there is no size A crochet hook anywhere on the planet.

You could spend an hour trying to memorize how the various hook size systems overlap and interact, but the art of crochet really doesn't require you to do all that mental sweating. How about this instead: Just go by the millimeter (mm) size of the hook, which is the diameter of

Better Shop Around

"There's so little equipment involved in crochet that it's worth it to find the right thing. For me, for crochet specifically I have to have the right hook, and there are so many different kinds of hooks that I think if I had been forced to use a hook I didn't like, I would have had a terrible experience. I don't like them too pointy or with little handles on them. Everyone's different. But it's worth investing a few dollars in a few different brands to see which one really fits your hand comfortably and makes you happy. To me that's a huge part of it: That ease and comfort and finding the right rhythm of it."

—Alicia Paulson, author and crafter extraordinaire, as well as blogger at her lovely website, Posie Gets Cozy (rosylittlethings.typepad.com). Check it out!

Think Again

You've found your best crochet hook. But then you start crocheting a lot and develop blisters or calluses. Time to reassess, says crochet artist Twinkie Chan, author of *Twinkie Chan's Crochet Goodies for Fashion Foodies*.

"If crocheting has become a big part of your life, treat your fingers and hands well!" she advises. "Is it worth your time and expense to explore a bamboo-handled hook, a polymer-clay-handled hook, or any manner of ergonomic crochet hook? *Yes*. Years passed before I caved and bought new hooks (the old ones still worked, why get new ones?), but my fingers are so much happier now!"

Chan says you can also modify your favorite hooks. "Make your own ergonomic crochet handle with cute rubber pencil grips and some masking tape to fatten up the base of your hook so that it fits inside the grip. Easy!"

Little bonus difficulty: Just for fun, it turns out that the millimeter sizes of different manufacturers may vary a tad. Is that weird or what? Lots of crochet work is pretty forgiving, so such minor variations might not affect your work at all, but if you are making something where the size is crucial, you gotta do that gauge check.

The chart below is kind of like a Fairy Godmother who has the flu. It doesn't feel up to bibbidi-bobbidi-booing all your needle-sizing problems, but it can help you see the correlation between common letter, number, and millimeter sizes.

HOOK SIZE TRANSLATOR CHART

Millimeter Range	U.S. Size Range
2.25 mm	B-1
2.75 mm	C-2
3.25 mm	D-3
3.5 mm	E-4
3.75 mm	G-6
4 mm	7
4.5 mm	H-8
5 mm	H-8
5.5 mm	I-9
6 mm	J-10
6.5 mm	K-10½
8 mm	L-11
9 mm	M/N-13
10 mm	N/P-15
15 mm	P/Q
16 mm	Q
19 mm	S

the shaft and is usually stamped on the thumb rest of the hook. Most patterns will include the size of the hook in millimeters, so you're golden. If it's an old or odd pattern and doesn't, you can use the chart at right as a starting point. You may have to also experiment with gauge (see pp. 18–21).

My Hook Disappeared!

Unlike knitting needles, which are big and pointy and believe in the buddy system, crochet hooks are solo travelers and masters of escape. They can slip away like magic sometimes, even while you think you are holding them. Now and then you will set down your work to leave the room, then come back to find your crochet work just as you left it, but the hook has hoofed it off to parts unknown. Really? Where did it go?

It helps to think like a crochet hook. A hook is basically an anchor. It is heavier than yarn and slippery, and it tends to sink. So when yours suddenly isn't where it is supposed to be, look down, look down, like Jean Valjean in *Les Miz*. Chances are it has fallen between the cushions of whatever chair you are sitting on, if not under the chair itself.

Here's a trick to make your hook sit and stay like a good dog: Whenever you set your work aside, thread the hook through the work a few times. Or stab it right into the ball of yarn. Make threading or stabbing a habit you never break, and you'll save yourself beaucoup d' hook hunting.

There will be times when you want to stick your crochet hook somewhere while your hands fix something, and the yarn ball is too far away to reach, and the most convenient place will be in your mouth. Don't. It's bad for your health and maybe your teeth and your work. Try behind your ear. Or, if you're wearing a bra or a watch, right under the strap.

Wait—I can't read what size this hook is!
Sometimes, for whatever reason, it's hard to see the size that's marked on a hook. Maybe the number/letter is printed too small, and you work in dim light. Or possibly the hook just plain isn't marked. You can solve the mystery by using a gauge measure/hook sizer to test what size your hook shaft is, and therefore what millimeter size hook you have. The gauge measure has holes in it, which can be used for either knitting needles or crochet hooks. Just dip the shaft of the hook into various holes until you find the one that fits. The hole you're looking for, of course, is the smallest one through which the shaft can be (gently) shoved.

Don't have a gauge measurer with its cute little Swiss cheese holey-ness? Use your tape measure or a ruler. Lay your hook on it perpendicularly and see how many millimeters wide that shaft is. It's not easy, but it can be done.

After you've determined what size this mystery hook is, you can be extra crafty and mark it in nail polish (or marker) on the handle if you like, to avoid repeating this measuring exercise for that hook again. Feel free to add a smiley face, too, or a little Elvis TCB lightning bolt, because you are taking care of business.

Safety Tip #3: Master the Yarn

A lot of us know the feeling Twinkie Chan is talking about in the sidebar to the right. You walk into a charming yarn shop like a normal human and walk out tipsy, besotted with the amazing variety of choices, bewitched by the sample projects draped about the shop.

But use caution. While there's no need to hunt down exactly the yarn suggested in a project's pattern, there are usually a few key reasons why the pattern designer picked it. We'd all do well to guess at what those reasons probably were when choosing a substitute yarn or even finding the one called for.

WEIGHTY MATTERS

The first consideration is **weight**, which you will find marked on the yarn label. Actually, there are two "weights" on the yarn label. One is what the ball of yarn weighs—not a real handy piece of information, usually. The other is the category of weight, in which "weight" means the heft or thickness of the yarn. The designer of the pattern you want to follow has specified a certain type and weight of yarn and a size of hook in order to make what you create come out at the desired size, with the desired look.

Yarns have different thicknesses and weights (it would get awfully boring in the craft bag if they didn't), and when a pattern calls for one weight, that's because it will give the finished item a certain look. It's not set in stone, of course. You can play around with it if you are careful about checking your gauge or if you are creating an item like some scarves or shawls where the sizing isn't crucial. But when you're evaluating which yarn to buy, it helps if you've got a general understanding of the types available.

Yarn marked 0 is basically a stringlike thread, good for making lace, and is referred to as "fingering 10-count crochet thread," and also

Whoa, Nelly

"When you walk into a local yarn boutique (not a chain store) for the first time, your eyes are going to pop out of your head, your jaw is going to drop to the ground, and you're going to want to touch and buy *everything*. But in the beginning, we always advise crocheters to put down the fancy stuff and stock up on the cheap, plain stuff (no fuzzies or pom-poms or hairy stuff or bumpy stuff). You need to learn how to see your stitches first, and for some people, this can take a lot of repetition and a lot of basic projects. Don't overwhelm yourself or your wallet when you're first starting. Keep things simple as a beginner and then raid the art yarns later!"

—Twinkie Chan

"lace weight." Teeny-tiny stitches and the resulting crochet work will look beautiful and take quite an investment in time. It's probably best to hold way off if you are a beginner.

The yarn marked 1 is referred to as "sock," "fingering," or "baby" weight, or also "super fine" weight, and it is going to give you the most drape you can get with a yarnlike yarn. It's just right for stuff like socks, thin sweaters, little

YOUR BASIC STANDARD YARN WEIGHTS

Actual Yarn	Numbered Ball	Description	Sts/4 in.	Hook Size
Lace	**0** LACE	Fingering 10-count crochet thread	32–42**	6, 7, 8
Super fine	**1** SUPER FINE	Sock, baby, fingering	21–32	B-1 to E-4
Fine	**2** FINE	Sport, baby	16–20	E-4 to 7
Light	**3** LIGHT	DK, light worsted	12–17	7 to I-9
Medium	**4** MEDIUM	Worsted, afghan, Aran	11–14	I-9 to K-10½
Bulky	**5** BULKY	Chunky, craft, rug	8–11	K-10½ to M-13
Super Bulky	**6** SUPER BULKY	Bulky, roving	7–9	M-13 to Q
Jumbo	**7** JUMBO	Jumbo, roving	6 and fewer	Q and larger

The gauges and hook sizes in this chart reflect the guidelines of the Craft Yarn Council of America (CYCA). For more information, visit their website: www.yarnstandards.com.

**Lace weight yarns are usually crocheted on larger hooks to create lacy, openwork patterns. This makes a recommended gauge range difficult to determine. Always follow the gauge stated in your pattern.

lacy capelets, and shawls. Again, pack your patience. The results can look so professional that nobody will guess you hooked it yourself.

Yarn marked 2 is what we like to call "sport" weight or "fine." It's sometimes also called "baby" weight, just like yarn 1. This type of yarn, which is twice as thick as a number 1 yarn, could be used for, say, crocheting Barbie® doll clothes or baby sweaters—something a little on the delicate side, but much more yarnlike than embroidery-floss-like.

The 3 yarns are called "light" or "light worsted" or "DK," which stands for "double knitting," not Donna Karan. It's getting a little thicker now, but still thinner in diameter and lighter than the basic yarn you probably picture when you think of yarn. This one is good for more baby items, including booties and blankets, but also for scarves and some light garments.

Then we come to 4 yarns, which are the most popular of the bunch for crochet and are known as "worsted." (There's nothing "worse" about worsted, by the way. It's named for an English village called *Worstead*, where folks were manufacturing yarn in the 12th century.) Worsted is also known as "medium" or "afghan" or "Aran" weight yarn. It's what you'd see in the majority of traditional crocheted items, such as afghans, hats, scarves, handbags, and sweaters.

The 5 yarns are called "bulky," no offense. Bulky yarn is about double the thickness of worsted, and so it makes things, well, bulkier. That is a positive quality if you want your item to be thicker for warmth or structure, and it also has the bonus feature of working up faster since each stitch is bigger. Bulky yarns are alternatively called "chunky," "craft," or "rug" yarns, as you can see from the chart on the facing page.

The 6 yarns are "super bulky," but also called "extra-bulky" or even "bulky," just to confuse everyone. It has a really cool dramatic thickness, not unlike a rope, and so it is great when you want to make something quickly where the stitches really stand out visibly.

Finally, yarns are "jumbo" but you might find them labelled "mega bulky" or "roving." This yarn is even thicker than the size 6 yarns, is not unlike rope, and is perfect for projects featuring big stitches.

RIP ITS GUTS OUT!

The starting point on a skein of yarn can be hard to find. But the thing is, it is in there,

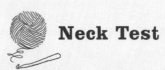

Neck Test

In Greece once, I met an old man who sold the most beautiful hand-dyed wool. I became enchanted by a certain blue he had, because I wanted to make a friend a scarf from it, thinking it would match her eyes. I spent the entire flight back home knitting this scarf, and then presented it proudly at Christmas, delighted at the way it made the eyes in question pop. Unfortunately, they were popping extra hard due to how incredibly itchy the yarn was. I'd forgotten to take into consideration that an item that goes around a neck should not drive the wearer insane. Strangely, the yarn hadn't felt scratchy on my hands at all the entire time I'd been knitting. So now when I buy yarn for a scarf, up to my neck it goes to test for softness, before my credit card comes out.

somewhere in the inner guts of the skein. So what I usually tell students is to stick their fingers right into the belly of the skein from one of the ends and yank a golf-ball-size wad of the most center yarn out. Don't worry if more comes out than you expected. Chances are you will now see the center end piece, and you can start forming a proper yarn ball to work from.

HOW TO WIND A PROPER YARN BALL

When I learned how to roll a proper yarn ball—one that has the yarn end you'll work with coming from the center of the ball—it blew my mind! Doing it this way not only looks better, but it also keeps a yarn ball from hopping all over the place, picking up lint and dust and tangling with nearby objects as you work. Super sweet! It took me a few tries to make the instructions I had read work well. Here are my tips.

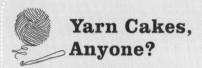

Yarn Cakes, Anyone?

A properly wound yarn ball is one of life's pleasures to behold. But if you wanna take your yarn admiration up a notch, you can buy a little hand-cranked device called a yarn ball winder. These fairly inexpensive machines look a bit like a hand-cranked apple peeler, but they rotate the winding yarn just right to create a perfect, flat-bottomed "yarn cake" (don't you love that term?) that feeds from the center. The finished cake resembles a ball of twine, and yarn pulls out of it with beautiful ease. Here's the plus: A yarn cake can be stacked on top of another yarn cake, making storing your leftover yarns so much easier and less messy than with the traditional balls.

STEP 1

Position your nondominant hand with thumb up and index finger out, and other fingers folded back, as if a gun. Let one end of the yarn hang down the center of your palm a good 5 in., then begin wrapping the yarn above it into a figure eight on your fingers. Do this about 30 times, and please keep it loose.

STEP 2

With that starter end still hanging down, grab the figure eight with your thumb and index finger of the opposite hand and gently lift them off your fingers. Then fold the two loops of the figure eight loosely on top of each.

STEP 3

This is the center of your proper yarn ball. Now all you have to do is loosely begin to wrap the remaining yarn around that little folded figure eight. Key element: Do not wrap too tightly, and keep the thumb of your nonwrapping hand poked right into the ball where the tail end is coming out. You want to keep that path marked and clear, as it eventually becomes the yarn's exit from the ball.

STEP 4

Keep wrapping until you get to the other end of the yarn. Abracadabra, you've got a beautifully wrapped ball, and you can now work with the tail end that comes out of the center of it.

A FEW WORDS ABOUT YARN COLOR

A pattern will usually specify a color, or a color range, as a guideline. But it's easy to fall in love with a different color once you're in the store. The only hard-and-fast rule on color is to make sure you get enough of the one you want. Even if a bunch of identical-looking blobs of yarn are hanging out in some basket in the store together, that doesn't mean they have

A Hank, a Ball, and a Skein Walk into a Bar

Yarn gets sold in three basic formations. Sometimes you buy it as a **ball**, with the yarn ends situated so you can work from either the one wrapped around the outside of the ball or the one coming from the inside of the ball. It's probably common knowledge that you should use the inside yarn, because then the ball won't hop all around as you're working with it, picking up lint and driving you batty.

Other times (and very commonly, for craft yarns) it's sold as a **skein**, which is a more bread-loaf-shaped oblong bundle. This is fine, too. No need to pull it all out and wrap it into a ball. Just remember to find and begin with the yarn coming from the center of the skein.

The fancier yarns are sometimes sold in **hanks**, which unfortunately have nothing to do with the famous actor of the same name. A hank is kind of a lazy arrangement: a loopy circle of wrapped yarn kind of loosely tied so it stays that way until you deal with it. And deal with it you must, because if you try to crochet directly from a hank, you will have a tangly mess on your hands eventually.

the same *dye lot* number and *color name* on the label, and you want to get that consistent. Just check to make sure you're matchy-matchy. And if it's for an important item like a gift, buy a couple extra skeins. Save your receipt to return the yarn later if you don't need it all.

THAT LABEL = YOUR FRIEND

In addition to telling you the weight and color name/dye lot of the delicacy in your hand, a yarn label gives you some other info. Namely:

Fiber content, usually expressed in percentages. This is where you find out if the ball of yarn is made from natural animal fibers such as wool, vegetable fibers such as cotton or rayon (it's derived from wood, believe it nor not), or man-made fibers, such as acrylic or nylon. Of course, if you're crocheting for someone with allergies to wool or other fibers, it's extra important to check. If you're deviating at all from what the pattern you're following suggests, or if you're winging it with your own design, the fiber content can give you some clues as to what the finished project will be like.

Washing instructions. See p. 16 for the lowdown on these mysterious hieroglyphics.

Gauge. Not all yarn labels specify, but some will give you an estimate of the gauge measurement if you use the suggested size hook or knitting needle (more on p. 17).

INTERNATIONAL LAUNDERING SYMBOLS

	Hand wash in lukewarm water only.
	Hand wash in warm water at stated temperature.
	Do not wash by hand or machine.
	Machine wash in warm water at stated temperature, cool rinse, and short spin; delicate handling.
	Machine wash in warm water at stated temperature, short spin.
	Machine wash in warm water at stated temperature.
	Bleaching permitted (with chlorine).
	No bleach.
	Do not dry clean.
	May be dry cleaned with fluorocarbon- or petroleum-based solvents only.
	May be dry cleaned with perchloroethylene or fluorocarbon or petroleum-based solvents.
	May be dry cleaned with all solutions.
	Press with cool iron.
	Press with warm iron.
	Press with hot iron.
	Do not press.
	Do not tumble dry.

Blooper Reel: Rotten Advice to Innocent Children

When teaching a group of elementary school kids to knit and crochet, I wanted to keep things very low-key. So I told them that for supplies they could bring in whatever color yarn they liked in about a worsted weight. You know what I totally forgot? A dark yarn makes stitches so so so much harder to see. And when you are first starting out, it's really important to be able to count and see your stitches, to check whether they went gnarly. It's also important to be able to see your stitches when you're more experienced, especially if you know you'll be working on the project somewhere like a poorly lit car during a road trip, or if you're trying a new stitch and are uncertain of yourself. Save the dark stuff for when you're feeling confident and have a good light handy. On the other hand, if you don't want the particular crochet stitches to show much in the finished project, dark is the way to go.

Suggested hook/needle size. Certain thicknesses of yarns go well with certain size crochet hooks. That makes sense, so the manufacturer will almost always give you a recommendation. Here's the catch: Some yarn makers are kinda blind to us crocheters, and only think of things in terms of knitting needle size. If you see only "suggested needle size," keep in mind that the millimeter sizes for needles are the same as the millimeter sizes for hooks. So just pretend that "needle" says "hook," then go by the millimeter size, and you're all set.

FIBER TYPES HEARTLESSLY STEREOTYPED FOR YA

It is terrible to stereotype. But having a basic knowledge of what fibers are like can be quite helpful when checking out the label on a hunk of yarn. Just keep in mind that most yarns will be a blend of these fibers, combining their pros and softening their cons.

Uh-oh. I can't find the exact type of yarn specified in the pattern.

Yeah, join the club. I almost never can, either. But it's easy enough to fix. The best thing to do is to ask for help, but only if you're in a shop where the staff is knowledgeable. In a big general craft shop, don't even try. Just eyeball the yarns you've got to choose from, looking for the ones that seem similar in weight and color to the yarn specified in the pattern. Now check the labels of the candidates. You may luck out and have a label that gives you not just suggested hook/needle size, but also suggested gauge. Match the gauge on the yarn label to the gauge suggested in the pattern. If there is no gauge, go with the hook/needle size. Remember, while a yarn selected this way is a pretty safe bet, it's still a good idea to make a gauge swatch when you get home, especially if your pattern is for something where the sizing needs to be precise. You can always return the unused balls of yarn if you can't get the gauge to cooperate.

But if I buy a different type of yarn, how do I know I'm buying enough of it?

Call up your phone's calculator function or get a piece of paper and pen. The label will tell you how many yards are in a ball or skein or hank, and your pattern should also dictate how many yards you'll need, via specifying how many balls of what yardage size the item requires. You just need to buy enough yarn yardage to match the yardage specified in the pattern. Then buy a little extra, just in case.

And finally, what is gauge, and do I really need to think about it?

Gauge is basically an industrial-sounding word that means "scale." The gauge helps you understand the scale of what you will be building with your crochet, so that you don't end up way off from the size you want.

Sounds impersonal, doesn't it? On the contrary: It's very personal. Because even if you and a friend sit down with the same type of yarn and the same matchy-matchy hook from the same identical manufacturer bought at the same time at the same store, your gauges can be different. One of you may crochet tighter than the other, and that can make all the difference. Left to your own devices, you alone may crochet tighter or looser at different phases of your life or different times of the day—seriously.

If you have a yarn picked out and a hook picked out, the way to test gauge is to make a gauge swatch. This is done by making rows of single crochet, back and forth, until you have a little patch of crocheted material that can be measured.

To begin, chain about 5 in. or 6 in. of chain stitches. Then do your first row of single crochet in those stitches and make sure the length is at least 4 in. long. If it is, continue making rows of single crochet until the height of the rows is at least 4 in. tall.

Now get out your tape measure or your gauge measurer or your yardstick or what have you, and lay it parallel to the bottom edge of chain stitches, parallel to the rows, on the little square-ish swatch you have crocheted. It is good to do this measuring in the middle of the swatch because stitches on the end of the swatch can be a little bendy and misleading. Count your stitches against the measuring

Pet Peeve

This is going to sound odd, but if you are making a gift for someone and are trying to decide on a color, consider the fur of the recipient's pet. A buddy with a light-haired dog or cat that sheds is just not going to wear the navy scarf you gave her, and likewise, the amiga with the black lab riding in the car all the time will have to put in some serious hair-removal efforts on the cute white crocheted handbag you slaved over for weeks.

Match the animal, if you can, or stay in the general lightness/darkness range of the fur. If there are multiple animals in multiple hues, just try to match the sheddier ones. It's extra thoughtful.

THE PLANT YARNS (LEAN & NATURAL)

Yarn Type	Pros	Cons
Cotton	Absorbent	Can show mistakes, can shrink
Linen	Nice drape	Wrinkles easily
Bamboo	Silky and sustainable	Swells in water
Soy Silk	Soft and nice	May drape too much for some projects
Rayon	Stretchy, absorbent	Scorches under heat

THE ANIMAL YARNS (BAD GIFTS FOR VEGANS)

Yarn Type	Pros	Cons
Wool	Good for insulation in heat or chill	Can be itchy, can pill
Silk	Shiny, lovely	Expensive, slippery
Mohair	Light and fuzzy	Can be itchy, sheds
Cashmere	So soft	Expensive, pills
Alpaca	Soft, warm	May be too hot for sweaters
Angora	Fluffy	Sheds a lot
Llama	Hypoallergenic	Expensive

THE MAN-MADES (YAY, HUMANS!)

Yarn Type	Pros	Cons
Acrylic	Cheap, easy to work with	Can look cheap, might pill
Nylon	Nice sheen, strong	Can be hot

Measuring Stitch Gauge Horizontally

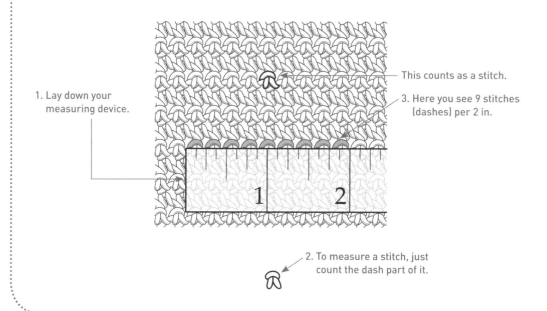

1. Lay down your measuring device.

This counts as a stitch.

3. Here you see 9 stitches (dashes) per 2 in.

2. To measure a stitch, just count the dash part of it.

Measuring Row Gauge Vertically

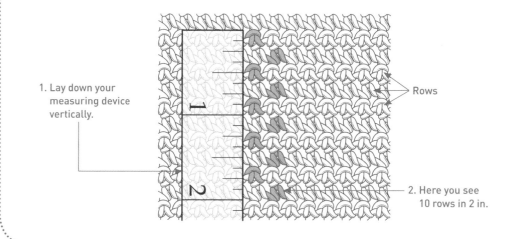

1. Lay down your measuring device vertically.

Rows

2. Here you see 10 rows in 2 in.

device to see how many of them fit in 2 in. If you have a half of a stitch at the end of your measuring instead of coming to a stop at a full stitch, just count that, accurately, as a half stitch. Once you have that magic number, you should double it to get the number of stitches in a 4-in. swatch, which is usually the number specified in patterns. Or you can halve it to get the number specified in a 1-in. swatch. Or whatever. You get the math.

Next, if your pattern specifies row gauge, do the same thing with your measuring device positioned perpendicular to the rows of crochet stitches. In other words, now you are measuring how many rows up and down make 2 in., instead of how many stitches across in the row make 2 in. Do the same thing with the counting of the half-rows if you need to; the idea is to be as accurate as possible. Then double that number to get the number of rows in 4 in., or divide by 2 to get the number of rows in 1 in. And there you go; you now have a measurement of the number of stitches and rows in a 4-in. swatch.

How obsessive do I need to be about this gauge thing?

It's more a question about how anal you can stand to be. If you really want to go the correct route and take no chances, before you measure your gauge swatch, you should wash it according to the yarn label instructions and let it dry. If you plan to block the item (see pp. 67–69), you should also block the swatch before measuring. Yeah, I know, right? A lot of us simply were not born with the patience, but it could be crucial if we are making a garment. In other words, it's another one of those kinda dull tasks that could save tens of hours of work in the end. If you are making a scarf or a blanket or something that doesn't really need to be that precise, or certainly if it's something that probably won't ever get washed, you can skip the washing step.

Great. My gauge isn't matching the pattern's specifications. Now what?

Grab some crochet hooks in different sizes and see if they make a difference. For instance, if you have too many stitches or rows per inch to fit the gauge, try making the swatch with a bigger hook. And if you have too few per inch, try a smaller hook. Keep playing, and you'll find the sweet spot. What you want to avoid is stretching or scrunching the swatch to force the gauge to work. That's a real quick way to fix things, and it's kind of funny. But it's also cheating, and will come back to bite you in the bottom. Protecting your bottom is the mission of this book, so we can't have that.

The Alien Language of Crochet Patterns

If you're used to reading instructions in your sensible native human language, a crochet pattern can be jarring. Suddenly you find yourself staring at hordes of abbreviations, as if there's a major vowel shortage, plus what seem like random asterisks and brackets. Chart versions of crochet patterns can be even more intimidating. To the uninitiated these look basically like a sketch of stadium seating and telephone poles, nothing more.

Fortunately crochet patterns are decipherable. In fact, they're awesome once you find their logic and hook into it, so to speak. This chapter contains all the low-down on crochetese, plus tips on picking patterns and dealing with their occasional flaws.

First Things First: Choose Your Project Wisely, Grasshopper

It makes total sense: The best way to invite crochet disaster is to do a crummy job of picking your project. If you get in over your head with certain stitches, if the project calls for yarn that's tricky to handle, if the thing you make has no prayer of getting finished in the next decade, well, you're just shooting yourself in the foot.

But what about when you see some crocheted wonder on Pinterest or in a shop and go into absolute raptures of project lust over something that might be out of your league? Is that bad? No! Project lust is good, always. Still, it's wise to step back a bit and analyze what's calling to you.

Really stare at the photograph or item itself (if you're lucky enough to handle a finished example of it) and consider a few questions:

- What's attracting your eye? Is it the yarn choice? The cuteness factor? The practical usability of the item? The color?

- What is the difficulty level? If it's a step or two up from what you've done in the past, do you have someone to call, Ghostbusters-style, if you run into trouble?

- How many pieces are involved in this project? Sometimes an item looks like one piece, but is really many pieces sewn together. Or the other way around. Better be down with that.

- Is it possible you don't really love this project, but you just love how it is photographed or the model it's photo-graphed with? Try to edit those factors out. Picture that fetching cloche on Homer Simpson instead of the chic hipster pictured. Still in love? If so, good sign.

Usually after a photo of a project, a pattern will include a paragraph-length description of it. Read this like an English lit major looking for foreshadowing, because it's the one place in the pattern where the designer is talking to you like a friend. She may mention a "deceptively simple" stitch, or a variation that could make things easier (or harder, if you're feeling extra capable). Look for clues like "foolproof," "fun challenge," "quick to finish," anything that tips you off to the emotions and effort involved. Combine this with the pattern's stated difficulty level to form your opinion about whether to proceed just now.

YEAH, AND HOW MUCH SHOULD I TRUST THAT DIFFICULTY LEVEL?

That depends. First off, wouldn't it be nicer if projects came marked with an ease level? Oh well. Instead it's the difficulty level, and before you check it out, get your grain of salt ready, because this is all subjective stuff. "Beginner" usually means it's super-basic and is safe for everyone. But since no Yarn Skills Adjudicator ever shows up to certify that you've improved, at what point do you know you have graduated to Intermediate projects? Plus, what if you possess the confidence and stamina to zoom straight from Beginner to Experienced in the space of a week? Such people exist. You could be one of them.

While resisting the urge to pigeonhole yourself too much, it doesn't hurt to be realistic. If you've got bucketloads of crochet cred but know you'll be working this project mostly in a dim car during the trip to Grandma's house at Thanksgiving, cut yourself some difficulty slack.

According to the yarn industry's trade asso-ciation, the Craft Yarn Council of America (www.craftyarncouncil.com, www.yarn standards.com), here are the guidelines for which level means what:

BEGINNER

Projects for first-time crocheters, using basic stitches with minimal shaping.

EASY

Projects with basic stitches, repetitive stitch patterns, simple color changes, and also simple shaping and finishing.

INTERMEDIATE

Projects using a variety of techniques, like basic lace patterns or color patterns, and also having mid-level shaping and finishing.

EXPERIENCED

Projects with intricate stitch patterns and techniques, such as nonrepeating patterns, multicolor techniques, fine threads, small hooks, and/or detailed shaping and finishing.

PSSST: HEY, BUT WHAT IS SHAPING? WHAT IS FINISHING?

Shaping just means you change the shape of the crocheted item by varying the stitches in a way dictated by the pattern, like increasing and decreasing. Finishing is whatever you do when you've got all the pieces of the pattern crocheted, in order to sew it up and make it look less like a pile of random yarn potatoes and more like a done thing.

Because not all crochet patterns come marked with difficulty levels, let alone ones that match the exact terminology of the Craft Yarn Council of America, you may have to do a little guessing. Knowing the bedrock definitions can give you a clue about whether you're going to be crocheting over your head (which sure sounds uncomfortable, but can sometimes be exactly the challenge your brain craves).

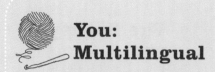

You: Multilingual

Gotta be honest here: Just because you've gotten through one crochet pattern with no problem doesn't mean the next will flow with ease. Even though there are standards for patterns, individual designers apply these differently. In some cases what you are reading may not make sense until you start trying it with your hook and comparing it to the photos. But if you have the basic building blocks supplied by this chapter, you can figure it out. And if you find a designer whose instructions make sense to you, stick with that designer for a while!

TODAY'S SPECIAL

One more place to check before you decide whether to embark on a pattern is a section near the top, usually right under the paragraph-length description of the item, marked something like Special Stitches. That's where the designer gives the directions for any stitch combinations that aren't basic. A habit to form once you're feeling pretty good about your crochet-reading skills: Run through this section mentally and see if that stitch sounds like something you'd like to try. Remember, you may be doing it tens if not hundreds of times in the pattern.

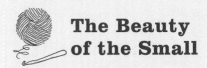

The Beauty of the Small

If you're feeling rusty or extra humble, choose a small (one ball of yarn or less) project to warm up with—ideally something you can give as a gift (like All Choked Up, p. 95). The pleasure of seeing that you can execute a small item beautifully without frustration, especially if you can really delight a friend with it, will motivate you. Also, it will remind you why you love crochet so much, and possibly even deepen the affair.

SAGE ABOUT GAUGE

Right up there on the pattern with the photo, yarn specifications, hook sizes, etc., you'll find your gauge section. In researching this book, I've talked to experts and read many an article and book about crochet. Gotta give it to you straight. A message rings forth from the sages: Don't you dare skip the gauge section of a pattern.

We went over this in Chapter 1, but it bears repeating. If you are making an item where size really doesn't matter much, such as some scarves and toys and household accessories, okay, go ahead, ditch the gauge. The worst thing that can happen is a redo, right? Likewise, if you're a renegade freestyle crocheter and are willing to throw in some design modifications of your own to make up for gauge differences and are comfortable with uncertainty, go for it.

But if you're making anything that really needs to look good in a fitting way, advance prep is pretty much required (see pp. 18–21 for how to measure and fix gauge). Eyeball the result and then, if it doesn't match the pattern's gauge, as Tim Gunn would say, "Make it work."

DON'T FORGET TO TAKE THE OTHER GAUGE, TOO!

What other gauge, you say? Well, the one that's marked something like "Finished Size" on the pattern, listing how big the finished item will be. It won't do you any good getting the gauge right if the size of the pattern doesn't work for you or your recipient. WARNING: The measurements listed under Finished Size will tell you the finished size of the item, not the size of the thing it is supposed to fit on. So if you have a 32-in. bust and make a 32-in. sweater, prepare to feel sausaged the one time you force yourself to wear it. A handy rule of thumb is to select the size up from the measurement that represents the body you want the item to fit. You'll need about 2 in. of clearance for something like a bust for a snugger fit, and up to 4 in. to 6 in. if you prefer more wiggle room.

What are these parentheses in the Finished Size section?
If directions are given for several possible sizes, pattern designers save space by noting them using parentheses. For example, "Directions are written for size Small (S). Changes are included for size Medium (M), Large (L), and Extra-Large (XL). These changes are in parentheses." Then you'll see something like, "Finished bust: 28 (34, 40, 46) in." In other words, the Small is 28 in. around, the Medium is 34 in., the Large 40 in., and the Extra-Large 46 in. Beware, because larger sizes may call for you to purchase additional yarn. I'm looking at a pattern right now where you'd be fine with

three skeins for the Small through Medium, but would need four for the Large. Following the advice in Chapter 1 (p. 15), you'd probably buy an extra skein anyway for possible later return if you don't use it, but if you read this part of the pattern carefully now, you'd know you need an extra extra skein.

THE SWEETLY CAUTIOUS NATURE OF CROCHET PATTERNS

What if you bought a computer program that allowed you to become a best-selling novelist? The way it would do this is by showing you how to check your work, at the end of each line you wrote, to see that you were still on track to write the next *Gone with the Wind*. Sounds magical, right? But crochet patterns are kind of built this way. At the end of every line of instructions for a row or round of stitches, a stitch count is given (well, in most patterns

it is, anyway). That's your chance to check to see if you're still on target, at least as far as number of stitches go. Pretty brilliant. And encouraging. Kind of like having someone hold your hand as you cross a street.

CLUES FROM THE SCHEMATICS

Before you bust out your hook and go wild on this new pattern, cast your peepers over in the direction of its schematic drawings (aka the schematics, which sure sounds like the name of an '80s band). Most patterns will have these: outlined plain drawings showing the shape of the finished pieces of a project, with measurements given for each size.

If the schematics show fairly geometric shapes with no curves, you're probably in beginner-level project territory, depending on what stitch is involved. The more curves and angles, the more adjustments you'll be making along the way.

Rookie Mistake: Shopping without Your Crochet Bag (Plus a Way to Avoid Bringing It)

It's always a savvy move to shop with your crochet bag, because then you know what tools you own. If a pattern calls for a size F/5 hook, do you really know that you have one at home? Maybe you think you do, but that's the one you dropped into that unreachable space behind the radiator. Also, do you have hooks a little bigger and smaller than the one you need, in case you need to adjust gauge? Knowing always trumps guessing.

One way to avoid lugging the bag is to take a photo of your crochet hooks before you leave the house, or keep a list of them on your phone or in your wallet. Just make sure when you take the photo that the zoom option on the camera allows you see the hook size markings.

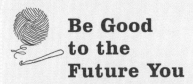

Be Good to the Future You

That pencil in your crochet bag doesn't look as fun as the hook, but use it to take notes all over your printed patterns, and you'll thank yourself in the future. Even just writing down what yarn and hook you used may save you a headache down the road.

The numbers alongside the schematics are usually in a format such as 7 (9, 11, 13). These correspond to the size garment you're making, so you have to deal with only one of them. Note that they can either be in inches or centimeters. Also note that it's a wonderful, great, mandatory idea, once you finish any part of your work corresponding to a measurement on the schematic, to be picky and do the actual measuring. If your work is off from the schematic's number, halt all forward progress. Something is wrong with your gauge, and it may be time for a do-over. Better to find out sooner than later.

SECOND THINGS SECOND: DOWN FOR THE COUNT

Okay, cool. Now we get to the directions part of a pattern. But to master that stuff, you need to understand your work, and this involves understanding where stitches begin and end.

Is that a "no duh"? It sounds so basic. It is possible, however, to crochet for decades while being illiterate in stitch ID. Many crafters think once the stitch is off the hook, they are, too; no need to inspect further except for the end-of-line counts if there's a concern. This is where we sail into choppy waters, because—true fact—the only way to crochet with confidence is to be able to police your work, noticing mistakes before they steal too much of your time and peace of mind. If you have a sense of what goes where visually, you're so much better off.

A SLIPPERY LITTLE FELLA

Riddle: What's the one part of a pattern that's always required but never mentioned?
Answer: The slipknot!

Before you chain the first stitches of a pattern, you have to make a slipknot to get the yarn on the hook. The slipknot does not get mentioned in a pattern because it is just the attachment of your hook to the yarn. Once you've got your slipknot on the hook, guess what? The slipknot is no longer the piece of yarn looped around the hook. It's just the little knot formed under that loop. And just as that knot gets zero credit in print, you also never count it as a stitch. It's just your starting point, not a star, handy as it was. Poor slippy.

CHAIN CHAIN CHAIN

The chain stitch is the easiest jam ever, and almost disappears once you've worked into it for the first row of stitches, correct? But to avoid confusion when working, from the front (sometimes called the top), each little V is a chain stitch. From the back (sometime called the bottom), each stitch will look like a hump.

Wag a Long Tail

A good habit to adopt, according Twinkie Chan, is to leave a generous tail (the end of the yarn with the cut piece) when making your slipknot.

"I always give myself a 12-in. yarn tail before starting any project," Chan says. "Sometimes you can use yarn tails to sew up weird gaps or holes in your work, for instance, from increasing or decreasing or working on both sides of the foundation chain. Sewing kinda feels like cheating, like maybe the pattern shouldn't have left holes in the first place, and now I'm just covering my butt, but, hey, if it closes up those gaps, I'm all for it!"

THE OTHER BASIC STITCHES: AN ID TEST

The most expert *artistes d'crochet* (plus a lot of skilled grandmas) can look at a crocheted item and read it like a book, seeing which stitch went where and why. Most of us aren't that fluent, but it still helps to be able to parse the basic stitches.

Notice how if you examine, for instance, a gauge swatch of simple single crochet stitches, they look quite different from row to row, though they are the same stitch going back and forth. That's just because a crochet stitch has a different look from the front and back. It's like you're looking at a stack of identically outfitted Radio City Music Hall Rockettes® all lined up facing you, with another stack of Rockettes with their backs to you stacked on top of the cooperative and apparently quite strong bottom row of Rockettes. And then another row of forward-facing Rockettes on top of that whole arrangement.

Your job is just to be sure you know where one row begins and another one ends, and to be able to identify which Rockette costume you're looking at as well as how many

Rockettes are lined up (and if you're working in the round, of course, all those Rockettes tend be facing the same way, unlike with rows). Maybe this analogy is getting a little tired, so let's abandon it and check out the following key features of crochet stitches.

It is also helpful when reading crochet instructions to know what the basic anatomy of any kind of stitch is.

Extra credit: Can you spot the mistake in the stitches in Basic Stitch Parts?
Hint: It's in the turning chain. Yeah, and I did it on purpose because I like it that way. See pp. 53–55 for why.
Note: If you need a refresher on how to make any of the basic crochet stitches (the half-double crochet, in particular, always escapes me before I remember what a cinch it is), see the Cheat Sheet at the back of this book on p. 119. Or go online for a plethora of filmed demonstrations. Some nice, clear illustrations and video demonstrations can be found at the Lion Brand Yarn website (www.lionbrand.com) and at www.craftyarncouncil.com.

Stitch ID for the Curious

SINGLE CROCHET (SC)

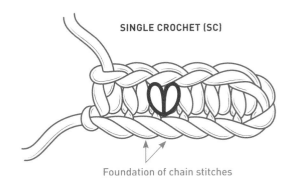

Foundation of chain stitches

All crochet stitches have a shape like this.

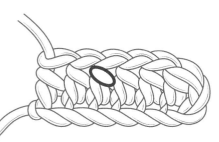

HALF-DOUBLE CROCHET (HDC)
Note diagonal slant of yarn on each squat stitch.

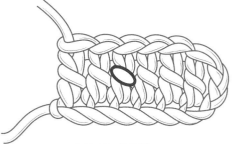

DOUBLE CROCHET (DC)
Double crochet also has the diagonal slant of yarn, but is taller.

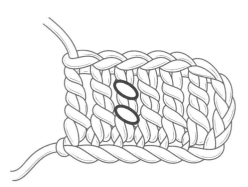

TRIPLE CROCHET (TR)
Triple crochet has two diagonal slants per stitch.

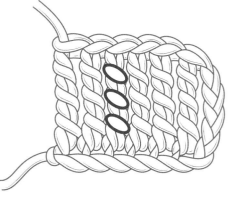

DOUBLE-TREBLE CROCHET (DTR)
Double-treble has three of these slanty things.

Basic Stitch Parts

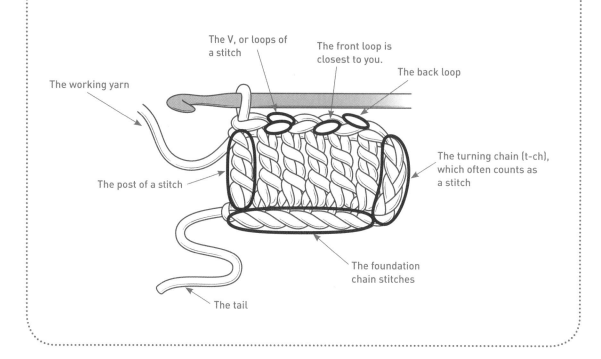

The V, or loops of a stitch

The front loop is closest to you.

The back loop

The working yarn

The post of a stitch

The turning chain (t-ch), which often counts as a stitch

The foundation chain stitches

The tail

One Pattern, to Go

Working a pattern out of a book but don't want to take the book with you? Copy the pattern onto card stock, then toss just those pages in your bag. You can fold the cardstock pages down the center vertically and they'll stand in front of you cooperatively, your instructions on display. This saves you from struggling to hold the book open on your knee to the right page. By the way, distributing copies to anyone is creepy and illegal. But if you bought the book, it's a-okay to make reading the pattern easier on yourself. Some crocheters even like to scan the text in, blow it up to a larger size, and print it out that way.

The Stress-Free Chain

Chaining the stitches at the beginning of a project is easy. It's the keeping track of them that's a pain. Say you chain 58 . . . or you think you did. Was that really 58 stitches? Or could it have been 57? You can count them again, but who's to say that new count is accurate? It can drive you insane, right when you need forward mo.

Crochet designer Sandra Paul, whose completely enchanting designs can be drooled over at sandra-cherryheart.blogspot.co.uk, has a suggestion for making this chain process less tedious.

"Basically the tip is to crochet too many chains," she says. "Very simple, I know, but it never occurred to me for ages. All you do is crochet the number of chains you need. Then, to save on the endless counting and recounting to make sure you're absolutely certain it's correct, just add on a few more. Maybe 3 or 4 for a shorter piece, perhaps a few more for a longer blanket chain, to allow for errors. Then you work your first row, just as you normally would. If all goes to plan and you counted right, you'll have 3 or 4 (or maybe more) chains left over at the end. If it doesn't go to plan and you need to use up a few of the extra chains, well, no problem, because there they are waiting for you! Then, to get rid of any extra chains that you don't need, just tease apart the original slipknot and unthread the chains one by one until all the extra ones are gone. You can then just weave the end in as you normally would, and nobody will be any the wiser!"

AND FINALLY . . . MASTERING THE LINGO OF THE CROCHET PATTERN

It doesn't take a genius to figure out that all those abbreviations in the crochet patterns stand for different stitches. While that's not what usually stumps people, it is annoying to be all juiced up for a new pattern and then realize you've kind of forgotten what a few of these little letters stand for. So here's the ultimate skinny. Hey, good news about the abbreviations!

Many of them are obvious (cm = centimeter; beg = beginning), and many others are simply not things you'll use that often (trtr = triple treble crochet). Within a single pattern, there probably won't be that many abbreviations to remember. A pattern that used even half of them would be an absolute train wreck. So you really only need to keep track of a handful on any given project.

Pattern Walk-Through

So let's pretend for a second we are starting a pattern. You've looked at the photo, read the description, decided it's right for you, determined your size, got the materials, done your gauge swatch. Honey, you are good to go!

THE CHAINING

The beginning of this particular yellow brick road starts with instructions about how many stitches to chain. Sometimes this appears before any row or round instructions, just on its own, like:

Ch 58.

Looks like it means Chapter 58, doesn't it? But no. It means put a slipknot on your hook (remembering Twinkie Chan's suggestion about leaving at least a 12-in. tail) and chain 58 stitches.

OFF TO THE ROWS WE GO

After you've done your foundation chain, the pattern gives you instructions for either round or row 1. Patterns worked in a row are worked back and forth, needless to say, and those in the round start with a circle and go around and around counterclockwise (for righties; opposite for lefties), with each circling of the circle counted as a round. Let's first assume our pattern has rows. It will say something like:

Row 1: Beg in 2nd ch from hook, sc 57—57 sts.

That just means you need to count to the second chain from the hook and start chaining across the row. At the end of it, you should have 57 single crochet stitches. Even if you use Sandra Paul's cool trick on p. 66 to make sure you don't have to be too picky about counting your chain stitches, you do need to count at the end of this row, and probably most rows, to make sure you are on target. Again, most patterns kind of hold your hand by telling you how many stitches you should be looking at when you reach the end of the row. In the above row instructions, it's the "—57 sts" at the end of the instructions that tells you how many you should have. But it also could appear as "(57 sc)" or ": 57 sc." This is not an instruction to do anything. It's just an accounting. You can tell

because of the way it is set off by the dash, the parentheses, or the colon, and also by the way the sc comes after the number. If the pattern wanted you to single crochet 57 stitches, it would say "sc 57" instead.

TO TURN OR NOT TO TURN: THAT'S NOT THE QUESTION

There isn't really a question about whether to turn or not to turn at the end of a row. Unless it's your last row on the piece, you're gonna turn, because you've come to the end of your assignment on that row. Patterns handle this instruction differently. Some will tell you to turn at the end of the row, like this:

Row 1: Beg in 2nd ch from hook, sc 57—57 sts. Ch 1, turn.

Others will stick that instruction at the beginning of the next row:

Row 1: Beg in 2nd ch from hook, sc 57—57 sts.
Row 2: Ch 1, turn, sc in next sc, *sk 1, ch 1, sc; rep from *—57 sts.

Still others will not even mention that you need to turn. But since you're on the next row when you get to the next line of the pattern, it's implied.

But what does turning mean, exactly?
It means you keep your hook in the work, but you take the edge of your work that's on your right, and you flip it so it is now on your left. Just like turning a page in a book. You were looking at one side of your work, and now you are looking at the other and ready to work across it.

Wait. I'm confused about which side of my work is the "right" side (RS).
Easy way to check! If the tail of your work is on the left, that's the "right" side of your work (i.e., the front side of it). Lefties do it the other way.

ABBREVIATIONS CHEAT SHEET

Abbreviation	Translation	Abbreviation	Translation
alt	alternate	inc	increase/increases/increasing (add to size of work by adding stitches)
approx	approximately		
beg	begin/beginning	lp(s)	loop(s) (the 2 parts of the top of a stitch)
bet	between		
BL	back loop(s) (a location on the top of a stitch)	m	meter(s)
		MC	main color
bo	bobble (a type of stitch)	mm	millimeter(s)
BP	back post (a location on a stitch)	oz	ounce(s)
BPdc	back post double crochet	p	picot (a type of stitch)
BPsc	back post single crochet	pat(s) or patt	pattern(s)
BPtr	back post triple crochet	pc	popcorn (sorry, a type of stitch, not a snack)
CA	color A		
CB	color B	pm	place marker/place a marker
CC	contrast color	prev	previous
ch	chain stitch	rem	remain/remaining
ch-1 or ch-2, etc.	designation of which chain or space	rep	repeat(s)
		rnd(s)	round(s)
ch sp	chain space (space created by a chain you did on a previous row)	RS	right side (meaning the front side of a project)
CL	cluster (a type of stitch)	sc	single crochet
cm	centimeter(s)	sc2tog	single crochet 2 stitches together (a method of decreasing)
cont	continue		
dc	double crochet	scdec	single crochet (decrease) 2 or more stitches together as indicated
dc2tog	double crochet 2 stitches together (a way of decreasing)		
		sk	skip
dc dec	double crochet 2 more stitches	sl st	slip stitch
dec	decrease (make work smaller by combining stitches)	sp(s)	space(s)
		st(s)	stitch(es)
dtr	double triple/treble crochet	tch or t-ch	turning chain
FL	front loop(s) (a location on a stitch)	tbl	through back loop
		tog	together
foll	follow/follows/following	tr	treble crochet/triple crochet
FP	front post	trtr	triple treble crochet
FPdc	front post double crochet	WS	wrong side
FPsc	front post single crochet	yd	yard(s)
FPtr	front post triple crochet	yo	yarn over (hooking yarn over top of hook)
g	grams		
hdc	half-double crochet	yoh	yarn over hook (same deal)
hdc dec	half-double crochet decrease		

Why do I chain 1 before turning?
That's called the turning chain, and it isn't always a chain 1. A row of crochet stitches has a certain height, and you need the space of the turning chain to get you to the right level for the next row of stitches. So you chain more (3) for double crochet stitches, and even more than that (4) for triple. With single crochet, the 1-chain-stitch turning chain does not count as a stitch, and with half-double crochet, the 2-chain-stitch turning chain also does not count as a stitch, but with taller stitches, the turning chain does. See p. 53 for a fuller explanation.

See p. 53 for a fuller explanation.

PUNCTUATION STATION
Hacked-off words in crochet patterns are fun and all, but pattern designers don't like to call it quits there. So they stick in some punctuation, too: brackets, parentheses, quotation marks, and asterisks that function like musical repeat signs, or a cowboy lasso roping groups of stitches together. Also, there are some semicolons and periods and dashes that behave more traditionally and punctuate.

Parentheses get used a lot, as we've already seen. They embrace the number of stitches in a row notation at the end of a row "(56 sts)," or

Continental Divide

I looked up some instructions for double crochet online, but the demonstrator was obviously doing single crochet. What gives?

She was messing with you. No. Not really. What gives is that British names for stitches are different from American ones, and some of the terms overlap. Isn't that special? It's as if Americans called Marilyn Monroe Marilyn Monroe, but the British called her Julie Andrews, and the person we called Julie Andrews was, in the U.K., Double Marilyn Monroe. Or something like that. No need to think about it. Just consult this chart if you're not sure.

American Name of Stitch	Equivalent British Name
Single crochet	Double crochet
Half-double crochet	Half-treble crochet
Double crochet	Treble crochet
Treble crochet/triple crochet	Double treble crochet
Double triple crochet	Treble treble

Why does the British system not have a single crochet, you ask? Well, it does. In British terminology single crochet is the slip stitch. Now you know.

Be Your Own Translator

Guess what: The instructions on your pattern are not a test. They are put forth to help you understand what the designer intended—that's it. Read through them before you begin and see if they make sense to you. Sometimes they only make sense to some of us when we have yarn and hook in hand and try it a few times.

It absolutely does not count as cheating if you want to put the instructions in a different format for yourself. Some crocheters have a friend read the instructions to them aloud while working (gosh, this must be a really good friend). Others transcribe them, row by row, onto 3x5-in. cards on a circular ring clip, then flip each card aside as they finish the row. It would be fine with the crochet police if you wanted to record a row into your phone and listen to it via headphones while working. Want to translate written instructions into a chart, or the other way around? Whatever floats your boat. And by all means, if something in a pattern is unclear, or if you find an error, leave a note to yourself in the pattern in case you ever use it again or loan it to a friend. And if it's possible, also reach out to the designer or publisher.

indicate which number of stitches go with which sizes, such as "ch 44 (48, 56)." If you came across this and were making the middle size, you'd chain 48 instead of 44, in other words.

Parens can also be used to show you that a series of stitches in a row is considered 1 stitch. So "(tr, ch 1, tr, ch1, tr) in 3rd st from hook," means that you work a triple crochet, then chain 1, then another triple crochet, then chain 1, then another triple crochet all together into 1 stitch.

Brackets show up, too. They can be within a set of parentheses, like "(dc, [ch 3, tr, ch 3] 3 times) in 1st st." Translated into English, this means, "Do a double crochet, then do that chain 3/triple crochet/chain 3 action 3 times, all in the first stitch."

Also super-important are **asterisks** (*). These mark a place in the pattern that the designer wants you to go back to for a repeat. But don't worry, the designer will tell you more. So you might have:

*Sc in next 4 dc, 3 dc in next dc; rep from * to end of row.

In other words, keep repeating that "single crochet in next 4 double crochet stitches, then do 3 double crochet in next double crochet stitch" all the way until you get to the end of the row. Often, but not always, the end of the part of the instructions that needs repeating is marked with a semicolon.

Sometimes there will be two asterisks to mark a place, such as:

*Ch 2, sk 1, dc in next st,** sc 5, rep from * across row, ending last rep at **.

That just means you do the chain-2/skip-1 stitch/double crochet in next stitch, then single crochet 5, and repeat that combination across the row, but you end the row at the part marked by the ** , without doing the 5 single crochets at the end of the row.

What if I'm working in the round instead of rows?

No worries. All the same symbols and abbreviations apply, but to begin the pattern, you make some form of circle—usually some chain stitches joined by a slip stitch into a loop (see pp. 56–57 for the basics and also how to do a "magic loop"), and then you usually use a stitch marker to keep track of where each round ends. You don't turn (that is, flip) your work over when working in the round unless it's a special stitch you're instructed to work that way. Mostly, you just go around and around and around.

AND FOR ALL YOU VISUAL LEARNERS OUT THERE . . . CROCHET CHARTS!

Maybe the tangle of letters and punctuation marks and written directions are just not your particular cup of chamomile. That's no problem! Some genius who deserves a thousand hugs came up with the idea of crochet charts, and they are the bomb.

Crochet charts work for people of all languages (usually following the U.S. definitions of stitches unless it's a U.K. pattern), and can be understood with a lingering glance once you get their symbols. They look like the finished item, because each stitch symbol looks like the finished stitch. For example, here's a crochet chart:

Yay for Charts!

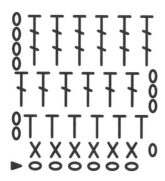

That might look like space alien chicken scratches at first, but consider this:

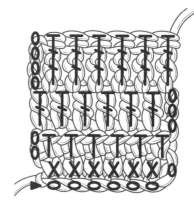

Here's how the stitch symbols got their shapes. Gotta love it.

Why Crochet Chart Symbols Make Sense

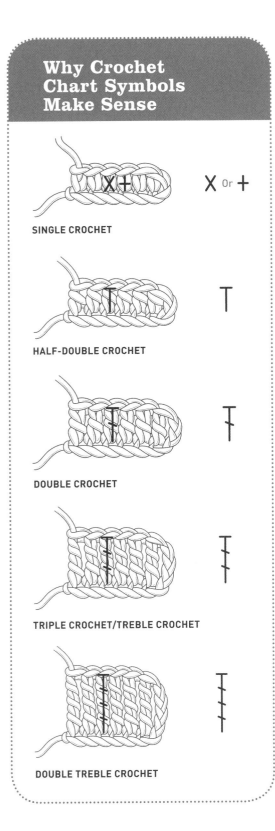

SINGLE CROCHET   X or +

HALF-DOUBLE CROCHET   T

DOUBLE CROCHET

TRIPLE CROCHET/TREBLE CROCHET

DOUBLE TREBLE CROCHET

And then there are a few other symbols that denote direction. Triangles that are shaded (it doesn't matter which way they are pointing) mean "start here." If the triangles are blank instead of shaded, it indicates the spot where you fasten off your work. Arrows (with a curve or without) show you which direction you should be working in.

The way to read the chart can be broken down into 10 steps. Remember that you are working from the bottom of the chart across that row and then across the row above it in the other direction, etc. These charts don't show the work being flipped. It's just something you're supposed to know, but it is pretty obvious. For left-handers, you might have to flip the image, but wow. Kinda genius.

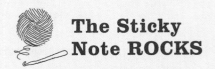

The Sticky Note ROCKS

You can understand a pattern perfectly but still get tripped up by losing your place in it multiple times. This can make you feel downright brain damaged. Here's the solution: Use a sticky note to mark where you are, moving it along as you complete each part of a line. If there's something you want to remember between one session of crochet and the next, write it on the note, stick it where you ended, and walk away carefree.

SYMBOLS AND DIRECTIONS FOR CROCHET CHARTS

✕ Or ✚	Single crochet
	Half-double crochet
	Double crochet (1 yarn over)
	Treble crochet (2 yarn overs)
	Double treble crochet (3 yarn overs)
◯	Chain stitch
● Or ● Or ⌒	Slip stitch
	Increase by putting 2 single crochet stitches into 1 stitch.
	Increase by doing above for half-double crochet
	Increase by doing above for double crochet
	Decrease by using 1 single crochet stitch to crochet 2 stitches together
	Do above for half-double crochet
	Do above for double crochet
	Single crochet in front loop only
	Half-double crochet in front loop only
	Double crochet in front loop only
	Crochet these stitches in back loop only
	Work these front post stitches with single, half-double, and double crochet
	Same as above but for back post stitches

Chart Magic

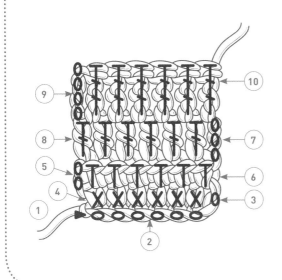

1. Symbol for "Start here." Some charts skip this.

2. Six foundation chain stitches.

3. Turning chain of 1 chain stitch.

4. Six single crochet stitches.

5. Turning chain of 2 chain stitches.

6. Six half-double crochet stitches.

7. Turning chain of 3 chain stitches.

8. Six double crochet stitches.

9. Turning chain of 4 chain stitches.

10. Six treble crochet stitches.

A FEW TIPS ON FOLLOWING CHARTS

Sometimes the designers mark all the rows in a chart with numbers, sometimes they mark just every other row, and sometimes they don't mark them at all. You can figure the rows out, though, if you know where the starting point is. If the starting point is also not marked, remember that for a piece worked in back-and-forth rows, the starting point is commonly at the bottom left of the drawing, beginning with the chain. And for a piece worked in the round, you start in the center and work outward in a counter-clockwise fashion if you are right-handed (you work in the other direction if you are left-handed). The little filled-in oval of the slip stitch in a circular pattern will often show you where one row is joined to the next, so that's another clue.

One neat feature of these charts is that designers can make the symbols in different colors, corresponding to the color yarn you are supposed to use. For lots of crocheters, this is a gorgeous economy of notation. The whole chart thing can come as a big relief. Or maybe it's not your preferred ride, because you like the words. The cool part is that there are options for different types of crochet readers.

AN IMPORTANT NOTE FROM OUR LIFELONG SPONSOR, IMPERFECTION: LEARNING TO LOVE THE FROG

Have you heard the verb "to frog"? Frogging means ripping out stitches you have done. It isn't difficult physically, most of the time. You simply remove your hook from your work and then pull on the yarn, and the stitches come

Why Are My Stitches Catching as I Frog? It's Driving Me Nuts

Yarn likes to get all friendly with its neighbor yarn strands, hugging them with tiny fiber arms we rarely notice. It doesn't want to be forcibly separated, especially if it is extra-fuzzy. Some yarns refuse to be frogged more than an inch or two without catching, which is why it's always a good idea to crochet a little test piece and then frog it before getting too deeply into a new project. Save frog-resistant yarn (not an actual term, though wouldn't it be nice if it were?) for items you know you can complete with little re-do. If you have a yarn that catches infrequently, but frequently enough to annoy you as you frog, look at the caught spot in good light, and you can usually tell where the fibers are banded together by fuzz. A gentle yank perpendicular to the band may be enough to break it free. Or you may need to very carefully snip the clinging fibers with scissors. A sewing seam ripper works well for this. Another tip for frogging happiness: Don't work near a shedding pet. Sounds gross, but sometimes those little catches are of pet origin.

Go Gentle

There's a price to be paid for overaggressive frogging. If the yarn catches on the stitches and doesn't want to come loose, you may find yourself yanking harder (especially if you're not relaxed enough about the whole concept of rewind, which is what frogging really boils down to). Be careful, because with most yarns it's possible to stretch the yarn fibers out so much via this yanking that the yanked yarn becomes thinner than the yarn still on the ball. If you frog and then use the thin yarn to crochet again, that section of your work will look wimpy. Should you find that you've thinned your yarn in this manner, there's bad news and there's good news. The bad news is, you've gotta snip that skinny stuff off and set it aside. The good news is, you can still use it for a different purpose: say, sewing pieces of your project together.

Watch Your Angle

When encountering difficulty in the frogging department, try pulling the yarn from a different angle. Sometimes that helps. Get yourself in really good light and look at how the fibers are gripping. But it's also possible that no adjustment of angled yanking or good lighting will help the fibers unbind. Oh well. You tried.

out one by one under the pressure, no duh. In fact, it is much easier to frog in crochet than in knitting, because you can do just a tiny bit at a time, without having to worry about long rows of stitches cast on the needle together. Yank to your heart's content until the badness departs. Easy, right?

Well, not if we're honest about it. Frogging can be emotional. You're undoing work you did on purpose, after all. Work that cost you time. Possibly you are frogging something you have already frogged several times previously with no success. Maybe you have reached the point where you would rather frog your own hair.

The thing to remember is that frogging is an honorable task, undertaken by crocheters at all levels of skill. It doesn't mean you failed; it means you have standards. How many forms of art allow you to erase mistaken work so easily? Precious few. So frog away and ixnay the self-flagellating, please. Yank with a sense of humor, which is how the term "frog" came to be, apparently: Rip it, rip it, rip it—yup, the sound a frog makes, and that's why it's called frogging.

It's super-helpful to be okay with making mistakes, which is why frogging gets included in this chapter about following patterns. This book is all about avoiding mistakes and mishaps, but when a boo-boo slips through, remember, it's easily undone. Froggie to the rescue.

TIME FOR A FEW MORE QUESTIONS

At one point my pattern tells me to crochet in the chain, and at another point to crochet in the chain spaces. Is that two ways of saying the same thing?
Those are two different things. When you crochet in the chain (ch), you crochet into the actual chain stitch, putting your hook between the top two loops of the V and the hump at the back of it. When you crochet into the chain

space (ch sp), that means to crochet right around the chain, enclosing that strand of chain with the base of your stitch. You don't have to get your hook stuck into the actual stitch.

This pattern won't tell me the number of chain stitches to start out with for my foundation chain. Instead it says, "work a multiple of 6 plus 3." Does that mean a multiple of 9? You wish. No, it means a multiple of 6 (like 12, 18, etc.) and then you add 3 more. It sounds crazy, but it will work with the pattern that follows that row.

Errors in the Pattern

Fact: Patterns do often contain errors. That sounds discouraging, but knowing that errors happen is helpful, because if part of the pattern does not make sense, you can remember it may not be your fault. Sometimes it's useful to fudge your way through the tricky spot and keep going, seeing if further rows enlighten you. Sometimes it's better to ask a crocheting friend for an opinion. If you do find an error, be a good citizen and contact the pattern designer. Most designers are grateful for a chance to improve their work— as long as you're nice about it, which, of course, you would be!

Even the Cool Kids Frog. Really Really.

"Sometimes the most simple-looking patterns can take *forever* to design and write, and that's okay! When designing and writing a pattern for something small and easy, like my Chocolate Easter Bunny Brooch, I might spend hours crocheting and frogging and crocheting and frogging before I can get the pattern close to 'just right.' Taking apart or throwing out days of work can be really frustrating and depressing and make you feel like a big loser, but your hard work will be worth it, and your care and determination will shine through in the quality of your work. I promise!"

—Twinkie Chan

I got to a row that says nothing more than "work even." What the heck?
Yeah, that's a weird one. It just means to work the same pattern in this new row as you worked in the one previously. It doesn't have anything to do with even or odd, or making stitches look all the same. Seems like that instruction could have used a bit more time in the oven.

When a pattern talks about the "right front" of a sweater, is that my right front, or the sweater's right front if it is laid in front of me?
When a pattern says "right" in referring to a piece you are making, it means the part that will go on the right side of your body. So "right sleeve" is the sleeve that will end up on your right arm. Same with left, only reverse that.

What does "break off" mean? It sounds brutal.
That's true. "Cut off" might be a better term, but no one asked us. The "break off" direction in a pattern means you have come to the place where you will stop using that yarn. While you still have the loop of the final stitch on your hook, cut the yarn about 6 in. from that loop. Then do one final chain stitch, pulling the yarn through the loop of the chain. Give it a little tug, and this forms a knot at the end of your work. All done for now!

Call me crazy, but I hate, hate, hate working the first row into the foundation chain. It's tedious and tricky. Is there an easier way?
Is there an easier way? There are multiple easier ways! Each has its pros and cons. The quickest fix might be to work that first chain with a crochet hook a size larger than the one you'll use for the rest of the pattern. For more ideas, keep on reading, especially pp. 44–45.

When Hooking Goes Haywire

So the first couple chapters have given you sea legs and a steady deck to stand on. This one is more about what happens when your Good Ship Crochet Project hits the rogue waves. Because I don't care how beginner or advanced you are: Every yarn undertaking comes fully equipped with "huh?" moments. Sometimes it just takes a little maneuvering or perspective to stay happily on course.

Foundation Situations

Crocheters tend to dread the second step of a crochet project: crocheting into the foundation chain. Not surprising. Compared to the other rows, this can feel like a chore, sapping your motivation just when you're getting started.

In Chapter 2, we mentioned a trick for dealing with the stitch count of that chain row (which helps). You can also use a bigger hook for the chain than the one you're going to use on the project, so the chain is nice and loose and easy to put that first row into.

Welcome news, though: These are hardly the only options. As many of us didn't discover for decades (insert resentful coughing sound here), there are actually four ways you can crochet that first row. Or five, if you count the magical one that doesn't even involve making the foundation chain in the first place.

The Full Credit is the one many of us are told is the A+ method. It leaves a nice edge at the bottom, formed by just the humps at the back of the chain. But getting that hook in the right place all the time takes some patience.

The Easier Way looks very nearly like The Full Credit when done because there's still one loop of the chain at the bottom of the formed stitch. In this case, it's the bottom arm of the V at the top of the chain stitch, instead of the hump at

Entry Points Galore

THE FULL CREDIT

Hook goes into each chain stitch below both arms of the V, and above the hump at the bottom of the chain.

THE EASIER WAY

Hook goes under the top arm of the V and the hump at back, and over the bottom arm of the V.

THE OTHER EASIER WAY

Hook goes under the top arm of the V, but over the bottom arm and the hump at the back.

THE HUMPFEST

Hook goes under the hump at the bottom of the chain only.

the back of it. No points off if you try this way. Give it a whirl. The only difference in the finished product: The loops of yarn at the bottom edge are a tad more slanty. It's pretty unlikely you'll meet someone who will notice that slight difference and be snooty about it.

The Other Easier Way is super-easy, because you're just slipping the hook under the top arm of the chain stitch. There's something to be said for the ease, but it does leave a little space in the center of each stitch in the first row, depending on what size hook and yarn you're using. If you try it and don't mind the effect, go for it.

The Humpfest involves simply crocheting into the humps at the back of the chain. It isn't as easy as the above two ways, but it is comparable to The Full Credit, and it leaves the sweetest edge of chain-stitch V-shapes at the bottom of your work. This is perfect for projects where you might later work a decorative edge around that work, or where you just want it to look neat.

LOOK MA, NO CHAIN

Create the first row of a piece of crochet without first making a chain? I didn't believe it at first. Then, after watching like seven YouTube videos, and consulting four crochet books, I still felt confused. Much research later, I've concluded that everyone should learn this method, because it makes certain shapes much easier to create. As an example, see the Times Square Bag on p. 100. The strap of this bag is formed by a no-chain foundation double crochet stitch. This allows the crafter to add length to the strap at will, without calculating how many chains it will take. You can make a strap like this in one row, and it has a finished edge on both sides. Genius!

Now bear with me while we make this as easy as possible, because it's fun once you get the hang.

To create a chainless single crochet row, begin by chaining 2 chain stitches. I know, I know: I said this was chainless. There are these 2 chains at the beginning, and you actually do make chains as you go, just not all on their own at first like usual. They magically appear as part of the first-row action.

So chain 2. Then, holding the chain horizontally with your non-hook hand, insert your hook into the first chain you made under the top arm of the V and the hump at the back, and yarn over and pull through, leaving 2 loops on your hook. Now yarn over, and pull that yarn through just the loop on your hook that's closest to the tip of the hook. This is the beginning of your chain row. See that little chain you just made with that last action? Pinch it in the fingers of your non-crochet-hook hand, and don't let go. Now yarn over, and pull that through both loops on the hook. You will next stab your hook right

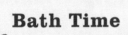

Bath Time

Unpleasant as it may sound, our hooks build up a level of grime and skin oils as we handle them, and this invisible crud can slow down the progress of the hook through its work (as well as being nasty). Try washing your hook occasionally with soap and water, then giving it a good dry. Some speed-demon crocheters even lube their hooks with a thin film of hand cream or oil.

Checking Your Tension

"You hear a lot of crocheters and designers talk about tension—and for good reason! The amount of tension you use while crocheting—holding your yarn and your hook—can affect the feel of the fabric and fit of the item. That's why making a gauge swatch is so important. It's rare to have the exact same tension level as the pattern designer. But it's not just your normal crochet tension that can affect things. Your emotional tension, aka stress level, can have a big impact as well.

"Ever started a project while you're nice and relaxed, and finished it a few days or weeks later while all stressed out? That project is likely to shrink even if you never miss a stitch. Getting in a 'crochet frame of mind' can help: Find a nice, relaxed spot to crochet in, make sure your shoulders aren't up around your ears, and find a hook that is comfortable to use. And if it's the project that's stressing you out, you can always send it to time-out and make something else in the meantime. Crochet should be fun!"

—Tamara Kelly, amazing crochet designer and blogger at the very fun and helpful www.mooglyblog.com, whose motto is "crochet • knitting • world domination."

into the chain you are pinching, at which point you can stop pinching it.

Important: When you stab into the chain you pinched, make sure you are putting that hook right under the topmost arm of the V of the stitch and *also* under the hump at the back of it. In other words, you need to stab right into that spot and also pick up the section of yarn behind it. Then yarn over and pull through that stabbed stitch. It's starting to get pretty now, and I promise it gets easier, too! Yarn over and pull through just the loop on the hook that's closest to the tip. That's your next chain, so pinch it and don't let go. You're just marking it with your fingers. Yarn over and pull through both loops on the hook.

The rest of this row simply repeats what you've already done. Put the hook right into that chain you've pinched, making sure it's under both the outermost arm of the V of the chain and the back hump, yarn over, pull through the stabbed chain, then yarn over and pull through just the loop closet to the tip of the book, forming the chain. Pinch that chain. Now yarn over and pull through both loops on the hook. Keep stabbing into those pinched chain stitches, yarn over, pull through, yarn over pull through the loop closest to the tip of the hook, then yarn over, pull through both loops on the hook. That's your pattern. When you reach the required number of stitches for the first row of your pattern, turn your work and work the next row as you normally would. Your first row may be a little bit looser than a traditional first row and chain foundation, but it's cute and also stretchy, which can be a plus in some patterns.

Okay, I get how to do a first row of single crochet without working a chain row. But how does it work for half-double crochet, double crochet, etc.?

Sorta the same! So for a half-double crochet foundation row with chain included, it goes:

Ch 2, yo, insert hook into second ch from hook, yo, pull loop up through that spot (3 loops on hook), yo, pull through just first loop on hook (creates chain), pinch that chain with opposite fingers to mark it and don't let go, yo, **pull through all 3 loops on hook**. The instructions in bold are the differences from the sc instructions. Then *yo, stab right into pinched stitch, same way, yo, pull up loop right through that place you stabbed (3 loops on hook), yo, pull yarn through just the loop on the hook closest to the tip of the hook (forming chain),

pinch that and don't let go, yo, pull through all 3 loops on hook. Just keep repeating from *.

For double crochet, it's ch 3, yo, insert hook into third ch from hook, yo, pull loop up through that spot (3 loops on hook), yo, pull through just the first loop on hook (creates chain), pinch that and don't let go, yo, **pull through first 2 loops on hook, yo, pull through remaining 2 loops on hook**. Then *yo, stab into pinched spot as you would for the sc method, yo, pull through just the first loop on hook, pinch that, yo pull through first 2 loops on hook, yo, pull through remaining 2 loops on hook. Repeat from *.

Triple crochet is ch 4, yo twice, insert hook into third ch from hook, yo, pull loop up through that spot (4 loops on hook), yo, pull through just the first loop on hook (creates chain), pinch that and don't let go, yo, **pull through the first 2 loops on**

To Have and to Hold

If tension is an issue for you—or even if discomfort is—why not get radical and try a new way to hold your hook and yarn? Some crocheters hold the hook from underneath, much as they would a pencil, while others hold it more like a knife for cutting food: from above. Try the one you're not doing.

The yarn hand (which is your nondominant hand) has many variations, too, none of them officially correct and sanctioned by the High Priestesses of Crochet. You can loop the yarn once or twice clockwise around your pinky, then bring the strand up the palm side of your hand and through the gap between your middle and index finger, then back over the top of your index finger, letting it hang down the inside of your hand. Or you can wrap it twice counterclockwise over your index finger.

You can also come up with your own wrap style, or a combination of these. Consider also the space between your hands as you work. Some crocheters run into tension issues when keeping their hands too far apart. Many of us feel better working with our hands so close together that the thumb and middle finger of the yarn hand is pinching the work developing on the hook hand.

hook, yo, pull through the first 2 loops on hook, yo, pull through the final (and only) 2 loops on hook. Then *yo twice, stab into the place you are pinching, yo and pull through the first loop on hook, pinch that to mark it and don't let go, yo, pull through the first 2 loops on hook, yo, pull through the first 2 loops on hook, yo, pull through the remaining 2 loops on hook. Repeat from *.

The pinching part isn't for me. Got another method?
Since crochet hook holds vary, some people might not have a handy pair of fingers free for pinching. You can use a stitch marker instead to mark that spot. But honestly, you may not even need to, once you get the flow of this method. Do a long row of it for practice, using stitch markers for several rows, and you'll probably be able to tell what stitch to stab into just by looking.

Keep in mind: Usually you can tell which side of your work is the "right" side by checking to see if the tail is on the left. That's because you've gone in one direction with the chain row and back again with the first row of work. But with these chain-row-free methods, the tail will be on the right when you are looking at the "right" side of your work, because you've only worked in one direction. For lefties, it will be the opposite.

That's all very nice, but every row of crocheting feels like a struggle to me. Is there an easier way to work the hook into the right places?
Whoa, whoa, whoa. Crocheting shouldn't be a struggle. If you're having a hard time getting the hook in, you're probably working too tightly. Maybe you are tugging on the end of the yarn after every little stitch. Stop that right now! Or maybe you're just in a tense mood, in which case you should take some deep breaths and calm way down. Try working with a larger hook and skinnier yarn for a bit, even if you don't make anything that way, just for therapy. The action of crochet is supposed to feel light and pleasant, almost airy.

Also, is there any chance you're working your stitches on the skinniest part of your hook tip, instead of on the rounded part? If you are working too near the tip, you'll definitely get a stitch that's too tight.

Misbehaviors of the Yarn

My problem isn't getting the hook in. I'm just having trouble keeping the yarn from splitting while I work. At least once a row a stitch is doing this. What gives?
This is such a common problem, and it never stops being annoying. Sometimes it really is the fault of the yarn, but sometimes it's a technique problem, or even a hook problem. If you're generally okay but have run into problems with this one project, it may just be a splitty yarn, in

Color Choices

Found a yarn you really love at some chain store? Guess what: There are probably other colors available. You just have to order them online (search for the manufacturer's name). The chain store is trying to guess what most people like, which may not be what you like. If you care about your yarn shop, let them know what you've ordered, so they can guess better in the future.

Color Changes: Must We?

For some reason, it is really hard to remember that color changes are often optional. If you hate doing them, think about it: Maybe you don't have to. Make a copy of the pattern's photo of the finished item, print it in black and white, and shade it with a pencil to show what it would look like in one color. Could be you like it just as well. Or try it with a variegated yarn and let the color changes surprise you.

which case you can either ditch that yarn in favor of another one or try changing the type of hook you use. A more rounded tip, or a more pointy one, may do the trick. Splitting tends to happen more when we rush, so slow it down if the yarn is misbehaving. You could also try a larger hook, but then you'd have to adjust the gauge.

One cool idea: Try working from the other end of the ball/skein of yarn. Really! Yarn is wound in a definite direction (you can see this if you look closely) and working from the other end of it can make all the difference, saving you much frogging. Naturally, this may mean you have to unroll and reroll your yarn ball, which can munch up some of your time, so test this method first before committing to it.

Is it really such a bad thing to have a split stitch now and then? Can't you just leave them in? You can. But chances are you'll be sorry. They're much harder to work into when you get to the next row, and a split stitch, even if it's just a few wayward tiny strands not being in the right place, draws the eye right to it when your work is complete. I have decided it's always worthwhile to go back and redo a split stitch, even if it's several rows back. It just feels better to me. You may feel differently, so don't let anyone strong-arm you about rightness and

wrongness. For me, it felt strangely liberating to simply decide I had a policy on split stitches. Not even sure why.

This yarn I'm working with isn't one of those fancy loopy ribbon yarns. But it refuses to be frogged well. Is there a fix?
Maybe. If you are getting irate and yanking really hard and fast, that may cause any yarn to catch. Try to pull your work out more slowly, allowing the fibers to unbind. Remember, they've made friends with each other and are all huggy-huggy. It takes them time to let go. But sometimes, yeah: Yarn is just too in love with itself to unbond when you ask it to, and in that case, the solution is to start over with a less lovey-dovey yarn.

My yarn keeps hopping all over the place while I work, sometimes spilling onto the floor, which was a lot cleaner before I got obsessed with crochet. Help!
See our instructions for how to wind the perfect yarn ball (p. 14), and then take that ball and tuck it between your knees while you work. This solution, however, will not work if you have either a cat or a small child who wants to keep messing with your yarn ball. In that case, you

may need to get protective and stash your ball in some kind of case. A lidded plastic storage container with a hole punched in it works great: Just thread the yarn through the hole, and if the ball is well-wound and has enough room to roll around in there a bit, the yarn should come out perfectly for you. Some people also use clean old tea kettles, with the yarn threaded up through the spout. How cute is that?

I've been crocheting just fine and am halfway through this sleeve, but suddenly there's an 8-in. section of my yarn that's totally deformed.

Thin and chewed-up and not at all like the rest of the yarn in the skein so far? That happens. When it happens more than a couple times in a ball of yarn, you should probably let the manufacturer know (via contact info on the label or online), as well as your yarn shop, if you think anyone there will care. To fix this situation, you're going to have to get all surgical here, and cut out the bad section and then rejoin the better yarn on the other end of it to the yarn you've already crocheted. For best results, do this at the end of a row if you are not working in the round. If you're working in the round, don't crochet right up until you're near the bad yarn; instead, stop while you still have a good length of tail to weave in.

When I add a new color in the middle of a row, my color changes don't look like the changes in the pattern photo. What am I doing wrong?

Maybe you're thinking logically, as in: Okay, I'm going to make the next stitch in this blue color instead of the green, so I'll finish this green stitch and then begin working with the blue. Makes perfect sense in real life. But in the crochet world? Think again!

What you need to do is start the color-change stitch during what still feels like the stitch before it. Wait until you have just two loops

of that stitch on your hook, then take your new-color yarn and, leaving enough of a tail to weave in, lay it gently over the nose of your hook (no slipknot needed), yarn over, and pull through the final step of that stitch you were making with the previous color. Make the next stitch in this new color, and you'll see why this method creates a pristine color change. You'll have to weave the ends in, of course, and if it's a piece that will be viewed from either side, that means leaving enough of a tail wherever an end must be woven in, and clipping the yarn that might be allowed to cross the color-change stitch on the other side, if that side is going to be visible. Just remember, whenever you change a color, do it in the previous stitch, for the step when there are just two loops of that stitch on the hook. Whether you're doing single crochet, double crochet, triple crochet, whatever, wait until the last two loops—that's the formula!

What about when the color change is at the end of the row? How come some instructions tell me to tie a knot and others act like a knot is the plague?

Different strokes. Neither way is really wrong. People learn from their friend or grandmother or some video online and think that is The Way. So try different ones, and see what works. Here is the knotless method that works for me: When you get to the last stitch in a row that has a color change coming up, wait until there are two loops of that stitch on your hook, then fold the new color yarn gently over the nose of your hook, leaving a long tail, and make the final part of that final stitch in the row with the new color. Then work the turning chain in that new color, and turn and begin the next row. Remember that knots at ends of rows are a lot less offensive if you know that side is going in a seam.

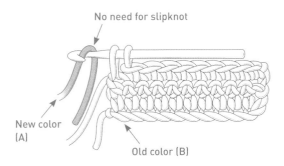

No need for slipknot

New color (A)

Old color (B)

1. Pull new color (A) through and complete the final stitch.

2. Then tug on A and B to tighten.

3. Work turning chain in new color. Flip work as normal to begin new row. Clip yarn from old color (B).

4. Lay tail of new color and old (A and B) across the top of your work and enclose them as you work across the row for 5 or 6 stitches. Clip them and keep going until they are hidden.

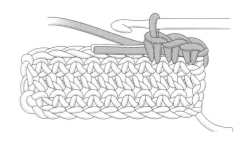

But you didn't tell me whether knots are the plague. Are they evil, or what?
They get treated that way. In general, the only knots that are approved for the proper way of crocheting seem to be ones that get tied temporarily if, for instance, you have to attach new yarn in the middle of a row—and then untied and the ends woven in. If you want to tie the end of the old color to the end of the new color at the edge of your work, you don't need a permission slip, especially if that edge will be hidden in a seam. You might try not knotting, though, and find the knot truly doesn't have much function. It's not like sewing, where if you don't knot or backstitch while making your dress, you end up nude.

That's the real skinny: Knots are rarely needed in crocheted work. They create unwanted bumps, and while they do hold yarn together, yarn will hold itself together when woven into the work or enclosed in stitches. Even when you change color in the middle of the row, there's no real need for knots. Just leave the tails hanging and then weave or enclose. If you want even more security, enclose the tails in several stitches as you work, then pull the ends away from the track of stitches so they aren't enclosed. You can use your hook or a tapestry needle to then weave them in.

If the knot is more for your own peace of mind, consider the slipknot option (see the first tip in the sidebar on p. 65).

I've unraveled/frogged some old crochet work and want to use the yarn for a new project. How can I get this yarn to unkink?
Steam! Steam is your amiga here. Take the curled yarn and lay it on an ironing board then blast it with steam from above, not touching the yarn with the iron (very important!). Straighten it out with your fingers a bit, blast more, and when it seems to be giving up its curl, you can wind it onto something flat like around a piece of cardboard or into a standard ball. Another option is to let it dangle from a hanger in the shower while you get yourself clean (if you feel that friendly with your project). The aim is to get those yarn fibers to relax. Maybe they just need to see a naked person!

I ran out of yarn before finishing my project, even though I bought the recommended amount. Really? How can this be?
It can be because humans are humans. Maybe the pattern had a typo. Maybe you read it wrong. Maybe one of your yarn balls rolled out of your

bag in that waiting room last week, and you didn't notice. Maybe your gauge is off. Maybe your math is. Any of these factors can result in a yarn shortage (or overage), so experienced crocheters do a kind of inventory as they work. When you're a quarter of the way through your project, have you only used a quarter of your yarn supply? If you're halfway through that scarf, have you really used half of those balls of chenille? You don't want to discover any discrepancies at the end of a project, because by then enough time may have passed that your yarn shop no longer carries the yarn you'll need (meaning: right name and dye lot).

My yarn shop no longer carries the yarn I need, and I can't find the right dye lot online, not even through Ravelry or eBay. What now? Creative thinking time! If you're working on a multicolored project, such as an afghan, maybe introduce another color, and possibly even undo some of your work to incorporate this color into more of the piece. For a scarf or solid blanket, you can add trim or a section of color at each end. If it's a hat, are you close enough to the end that you really don't need the rest of your yarn? Maybe it's just a less brow-grazing hat, or maybe—surprise!—it's now for the neighbor's baby you don't even like that much.

Another solution: Loosen up. Even if you can't find the exact dye lot, you may be able to find one that's pretty darn close. In fact, you might be able to find a totally different brand of yarn that's a near match (just make sure it's the same gauge and has the same washing instructions). If it's close but not close enough to fool the eye, you can go for an ombre blurring of the difference by frogging your work a bit and alternating rows of old yarn and new yarn before switching to the new yarn.

Yikes! Lost in Space!

You're cruising along, understanding your pattern, doing what must be done, digging it. But then you get interrupted . . . and when you come back it seems like some reset button has been pushed on the crochet area of your brain. You can't remember where you were in your pattern. You try to count the rows, and they all seem to blend together. Suddenly it's like being unable to read. Should you frog and start over, just so you can find your place again? No. No, you should not. Well, sometimes you may have to. But usually there's a way around it.

WHAT ARE YOU LOOKIN' AT?
The thing about crochet is, if you are working back and forth, one row and then the next, and using the same stitch the whole time, the basic crochet stitches (single crochet, half-double crochet, double crochet, treble crochet) do not appear the same from row to row when viewing the work from one side. In other words, a single crochet stitch looks one way on one side and a different way on the other side, and because you are going back and forth, the rows differ in appearance. So if you get lost in your piece and need to count rows, it's very handy to recognize what individual rows look like. That way you can tell them apart.

It's also good to be generally familiar with the shape of a stitch so you can tell where one ends and another begins across the row. Personally, I love how all the stitches are topped by a little chain-stitch shape. Not sure how many stitches are in that row you just worked? Count the chain-stitch shapes at the top of the row.

Really desperate move that also works: Sometimes if I'm lost in a piece, or can't tell where the increases are, and I've counted a row a couple times by hand but don't feel confident I've got it right, I resort to the following trick. Get some sewing pins, and stab one into each stitch in the row, putting two where an increase

One Cure for Loneliness . . . and Stuckness

Are you one of those crochet people who likes the idea of crocheting in some kind of craft group, except you don't have time for it? Try a Crochet-A-Long!

A Crochet-A-Long is when a group of people work on the same project at the same time, tackling a step of it in the same time period, and then moving on to the next step in the next time period. It's a great way to stay on track with a project, compare results, and feel connected. Search "Crochet-A-Long" or "CAL Crochet" online and you'll see a lot of options: afghans, shawls, any kind of anything. What a cozy, measured way to approach crochet.

is. For some reason, it is easier to count pins than to count stitches, at least for me. And then I can double-count as I remove the pins.

The scarf I'm working on keeps getting narrower. I frog and fix it, and then it gets wider. How can I get a grip on this issue without burning my vision out?

Stitch markers, baby! You'll need two, and remember that it's important that they be the kind that open up, not the little circles knitters use. Safety pins are a-okay, too, especially the ones without the circle coil at the base (because that can get caught in your yarn). Many other substitutes will work great, too.

Work your first row (after the foundation chain), and at the end of it place the stitch marker at the top of your last stitch (if it's single crochet) or at the top of the turning chain you make after that last stitch (if it's half-double crochet or taller). Then work across that next row and do the same with the second stitch marker. When you work across that next row and get back to the place where your first marker is, move it up to the corresponding spot on the row above it. Moving the marker is an extra step on each row, but it saves so much time in counting and recounting, and it allows you to be a more eyes-up crocheter.

Mysteries of the Turning Chain (and Some Blasphemy!)

To understand stitch count in crochet, and to keep your edges even, you have to understand the whole turning chain situation, which varies with the type of stitch you are using. Every crochet book will tell you that. What they won't all tell you is this: Some of the turning chain "rules" are bendable.

The standard line is that when you come to the end of a row of single crochet, you chain **one** to form the turning chain; in other words, the 1-chain length of work that allows your yarn to reach the height it needs to work evenly across the first row. When you are working in half-double crochet, you get to the end of the row and chain **two**, since it takes a height of 2 chain stitches to get you up where you need to be for half-double crochet. For double crochet, it is **three**, and for triple crochet it is **four**.

You definitely do need to crochet 1 chain stitch at the end of a row of single crochet, no argument there. If you don't, the edges of your work will get all sloppy. And for half-double crochet, yes, 2 is perfect. But here's the blasphemous suggestion: You don't really need 3 for double crochet, or 4 for triple crochet, like everyone tells you. Really. This is your piece of work, and you may try it with 2 (gasp!) for double crochet, or 3 (gasp again!) for triple crochet and find that you like the result just as much, or better.

The advantage to breaking the law this way is that it's incredibly easy to remember that single crochet has a turning chain of 1, double of 2, and triple of 3. Again, it's your work: Figure out what length of turning chain you like, then do that.

FURTHER BLASPHEMY TO SAVE FURTHER AGONY

Most crochet instructors tell you that if you are working a neat row of single crochet, back and forth, you do the turning chain and then single crochet into each of the single crochet stitches in the previous row. You also use all the half-double crochet stitches in the previous rows when working back and forth in half-double crochet. *But* when you work back and forth in this way with double and triple crochet, you have to do an extra couple of steps to make things come out even. Namely, you count your turning chain as the first stitch in the row, then skip putting a stitch into the first stitch of the previous row, then make up for that by adding a stitch into the turning chain that forms the last stitch in the previous row.

You certainly can do it that way. It works out numerically, with the same number of stitches in each row. But (one more time: gasp!) you don't have to. Ha ha!

Try this instead: With double crochet, crochet 2 for your turning chain (or 3 if you want to be traditional—it doesn't matter as long as you're consistent) and then DO work that double crochet right into the first stitch in that new row (oh my!), just as you would do with single crochet. When you get to the end of the row, also treat it as you would with single crochet. Don't even think about the turning chain. Just put your last double crochet in the final double crochet in the previous row. Guess what: You still have the same number of stitches in that row, and you have avoided the weird gap that forms when you skip the first stitch, plus you don't have to stab your hook into the tiny annoying place on the turning chain where you have to stab it to make that final stitch in the row work. You aren't even dealing with the turning chain. This also works with triple crochet. And even though some granny-square-makin' grannies may flip in their graves, the world does not end.

But if I like the "right" way of doing rows of double crochet, is there a way to close up those gaps at the ends of the rows? You betcha! It's a method for pretty much tethering the turning chain to the stitch next to it. After you make your turning chain, put the hook into the second chain from the hook and yarn over and pull up a loop (2 loops on the hook). Next, without yarning over as you would usually do, insert your hook into the place where you would make your next crochet stitch (the second stitch in that row, skipping the first one) and yarn over and pull up a loop (3 loops on hook), then finish that double crochet stitch as you usually would (yarning over and drawing through the 2 loops on your hook, then doing that again). Of course, if you are doing this, you really need a turning chain of 3, not 2, so stay traditional on this one.

I'm working in the round in a spiral (without slip-stitching the end of the round to the beginning of it) and can't tell where one round ends and another begins.

Place a stitch marker either in the last stitch of the round after you've finished it or in the first stitch of the next round. Choose one of these options and then forget the other way ever existed, because the important thing is to be consistent. If you are a beginner at working in the round in a continuous spiral, you may even want to leave your stitch markers in as you work. This will help you see how many rounds you've completed. It's also kind of cool to see how the beginning of each row migrates in a spiral, especially when increases are involved.

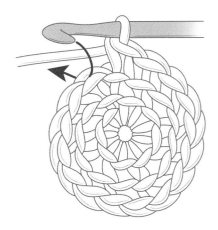

The stitches are worked into only the back arms of the V at the top of the stitch. See the neat track?

Option: Some people use a single length of yarn instead of stitch markers for this.

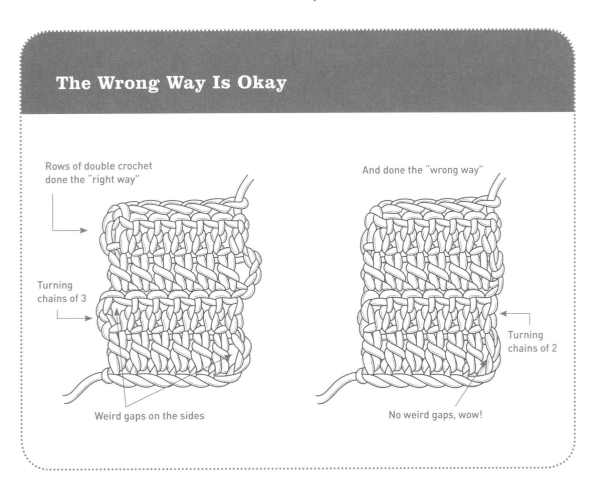

The Wrong Way Is Okay

Rows of double crochet done the "right way"

Turning chains of 3

Weird gaps on the sides

And done the "wrong way"

Turning chains of 2

No weird gaps, wow!

I'm not doing the marker thing. It just doesn't mesh with my personality type. Isn't there some easier cheat for seeing my spiral work better? Let's lose the word *cheat*. It isn't cheating to use tools to mark where you are, any more than it's cheating to have a speed gauge on your car when you're driving. But there is a trick for making the stitches in a spiral-worked piece more visible: Crochet each stitch into the back arm of the V at the stop of the stitch only, leaving the front loop free. This will give you a little railroad track of stitch edges you can see and count much more easily. It does affect your outcome a bit, as the circle gets larger faster, and is more flexible. But that may be exactly what you're looking for. Give it a try.

Speaking of crocheting in the round, my pattern says I should start by using the "magic loop" method. What the heck, and do I have to? You have full permission to ignore that and form the circle at the beginning of your work any old way you want to. But you should know why a magic loop (also known as an adjustable ring) is designated. Usually it's so you won't have a visible hole in the center of your circle. To form the initial circle of your work when crocheting in the round, you can chain 2 for a single crochet round, 3 for half-double crochet, 4 for double crochet, or 5 for triple crochet, then work the desired number of stitches for the first round into the first chain you made, the farthest from the hook. Or you can make a little circle of chain stitches: Say, chain 4 (depends how big you want your hole to be), join into a circle with a slip stitch, then work your first round into the circle you've just made. Or you can use the magic loop method. Here's the easiest magic loop we know.

1. Leaving enough of a tail, make a loop where the tail end crosses behind the yarn ball end.

2. Pinch this loop with your non-hook hand, setting the yarn on this hand however you normally would for crocheting.

3. Insert the hook through the loop, yarn over, and pull through.

4. Yarn over again and do a chain stitch (or more than one if your stitch is half-double crochet, double crochet, or triple crochet), as this is your turning chain.

5. Dip the hook into the center of the loop and crochet stitches of the first round into it.

6. While holding on to the last stitch in the round, pull on the tail. The hole closes up!

BONUS: AN EVEN EASIER FAUX MAGIC LOOP

Check it out. Chain 4, join with slip stitch to form circle. Now do 8 single crochet into the circle you've just formed, BUT, hang on, while you are doing that, lay the tail of your project behind the ring of the circle of chain stitches,

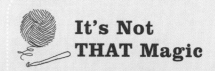

It's Not THAT Magic

Hey, kids: When using the magic ring, make sure you weave in the starting tail of it very securely after finishing your piece. If you just trim that thing off too short, guess what, more magic: Your ring can come undone.

so that it, too, gets enclosed in the single crochet stitches that are going around the round. When you have finished this round, grasp the work with one hand and pull on the tail with the other. Did the hole close up, or what? It did, because you made your own drawstring, which is all a magic loop is.

No joke, I made up this generic-brand magic loop while working on the instructions for the regular magic loop. Bet you can make up your own version, too, if you really need to. Not everyone does!

Unlike the photos in the pattern, the "flat" circles I am crocheting in the round for this project are not lying flat. They keep curling up like bowls. Why?
Basically, it's because your circle wants more stitches in certain rounds. The curling happens when a round isn't big enough. This makes sense, because a circle with no increases would be like a stack of identical bracelets and thus a tube. There is a formula for making a flat circle; did you know? For single crochet, for instance, take the number of stitches in the first round (usually something like 6 or 8) and add that number to each round. It usually ends up something like this: first round, 6 sts; second round, sc 2 in each st (12 sts); third round, sc, then sc 2 in each st (18 sts); fourth round, sc 2, then sc 2 in each st (24 sts); fifth round, sc 3, then sc 2 in each st (30 sts), etc. If your work is curling, see if your pattern is telling you to increase at a uniform rate like that, and make sure you're following its instructions. If you are and you're still curling, and the pattern is simple enough that this won't throw a wrench in things, look for rounds where the stitches are starting to curl, and frog back to there and add extra stitches in at regular intervals.

Experimenting will get you the result you want, and if not, see p. 80 for some helpful tweaks.

Note: Read patterns that call for crocheting in the round extra carefully, because sometimes the designer wants you to keep working in one direction, and other times she wants you to make a turning chain and flip your work, just as you would with regular crochet. Makes a diff!

COUNT DRAGULA
Alas, even when you've got your stitch markers going, or have mastered seeing stitches well enough to tell whether the sides of your work are as even as you want them to be, there are many other ways to lose count when following a pattern. So here are three more ideas for keeping it real:

More stitch markers. No rule states that you can only use stitch markers to keep track of where you're working at the moment. In crochet, these markers—or just a scrap of yarn knotted loosely at a certain spot and removed later—can mark your increases or decreases, places where you want to sew something, or even intervals in a long count. Think of them as being like a highlighter to call out important text. Let them help you as much as they can.

Paper and pencil. It sounds a little old-lady (and what's the matter with that, we ask?), but some crocheters work much better when keeping track of where they are on a sheet of paper, or on the pattern. Check off rows with a pencil. Move a sticky note as you go, as we've suggested earlier. Write down questions to ask a more experienced friend. Don't be afraid, in other words, to take notes.

If you find you have more stitches in a row than you should have, inspect especially the beginnings and endings of the row, because that is where stitches usually get added. Actually, this is also where stitches often get subtracted. It's a really good idea, especially when you are beginning, to be pretty obsessive about counting your stitches with each row until your eyeball gets more expert at assessing crochet.

With that said . . . some of our early mistakes at the edges of works in progress really do teach us how increases and decreases affect the shape of a piece of work. So if you make a mistake, take a minute to look at it before redoing it. The thing you just did accidentally may be the very thing you want to do on purpose at some point in the future.

HOW TO GET GREENER GRASS

Maybe you follow all the directions on a pattern, no problem, and you work with the exact yarn and hook recommended, and your gauge is for sure correct, because you've checked it three times, and you finish your project and . . . hey . . . it's nice, but it just doesn't look as good as the project looked in the picture that came with the pattern. In that picture, it looks as if it were crafted by magical fairies, while your finished thing looks very much mortal-made. Or maybe even troll-formed. Or the photo looks like it was done by a Ph.D. in Yarn Studies, and yours looks like possibly a high school sophomore was involved—A for effort, no obvious problems, but not a Ph.D., not that level of confidence. What's going on?

Several possible issues come to mind. One is styling. A photograph in a crochet book or with a pattern online is usually styled to within an inch of its life, using the best lighting and the specific angle that's most flattering. We can call this the Instagram effect. Someone has filtered it or edited it so it looks better than it does in real life. Yours might look exactly as good if photographed that way. You might even try a few pictures to see if this is the case.

A second issue could be tension/hook size. A bigger hook than the pattern calls for can give some crocheted pieces extra flexibility and drape, which can make the difference between a project that looks professional and one that looks a little too homemade. Sure, you used the hook required for the gauge, but it might be worth experimenting with a bigger one to see if your project blossoms into something lovelier. Similarly, if the finished piece is supposed to be very crisp with stiff structure, it might be worthwhile to play with a smaller hook.

It also could be that the crocheter of the piece in the photo has more experience than you do with keeping the tension of stitches uniform. What can you do about this other than crochet more so you improve? Well, you can block the piece. See pp. 67–70 for a few ways to do this. Blocking makes an amazing difference, even though at first it is hard to detect what that difference is just by glancing. You can bet your bottom dollar a properly styled piece in a crochet pattern photo has probably been blocked in some way.

Another sneaky possibility: The piece in the photo may be crocheted with a better quality of yarn than the pattern recommends. Better yarn does improve the look of a piece, no question, and sometimes a crochet designer uses that better yarn for the item but then is motivated to recommend a brand of yarn that is easier for the average crocheter to lay her hands on. Look closely at the texture of the yarn on both your piece and the photograph to see if this might be true. If so, try the project next time with a better yarn. Your local yarn shop can help you find an equivalent that's more luxe.

A final thought: You may just be mental, no offense. In other words, you can't see the beauty of your own work right now because . . . it's your own work. We can be hard on ourselves and can focus on flaws nobody else will see. Chances are when you look at this project in a month or two, you'll feel the wow effect. You may be too close to it to be properly amazed right now. Your grass is plenty green. You're simply seeing someone else's grass as greener.

Finishing Fiascos and How to Dodge Them

Y ou've crocheted some chunks of something, and you've done quite well. Excellent. Now it's time to stitch your chunks together and neaten up any stray ends, so they look like more than the sum of their chunks. Easy peasy. What could go wrong?

Stuff. Stuff can always go wrong, in ways both entertaining and very much not. With that in mind, enjoy the following platter of wrap-it-up-and-call-it-done strategies. They'll keep finishing from finishing you off.

Cut!

My pattern says "break off yarn" at the end of my work, but I'm confused about what to do with my last stitch before I do that.

Ah. Well, you can snip the yarn with a long-enough tail and remove your hook and pull on the loop that was on the hook until the tail comes through. Or you can snip the yarn, yarn over while the hook is still in, pull the cut end through with the hook, and then move on. The difference between the two methods is that the second one, the "correct" method for finishing a piece, creates a nice locked stitchy thing at the end of your work so it won't unravel. Frankly, if you do it the first way, it probably won't unravel either (assuming you're still going to finish the edge where it is in some way and not just leave it flapping in the breeze), unless someone picks at it. But in general, it's better to do it the second way, just to be sure. And incidentally, it's a cinch to undo that locked stitch if you find it is getting in your way or if you need to go back and correct a mistake. Just loosen the little loop around the cut end strand of yarn, and then pull that strand out of the center of the loop.

The End . . . for the Ends

I admit it: When I first started crocheting, I had no idea what to do with the tail and the various ends that hung off my work wherever I'd added new yarn or ended old yarn.

I knew they shouldn't be there—because they looked stupid—but it didn't occur to me there were special ways to make them vanish. Since my background was in sewing, I figured I'd tie a knot in them and cut them off. Except, huh, now those knots and little stubs of tails looked pretty dumb, too. Oh well! On to the next project.

Of course, if you know anything about crocheting, you are probably shaking your head at my ignorance. Because many a generation of crocheters before me had already discovered that yarn is kinder than thread. It has grippy qualities that allow it to be hidden among other yarn, no knot required, forever.

But where are these wise ancestors of crochetdom when you come to the part of the pattern that says, "Weave in ends"? That's right. Silent. In most patterns, it's just assumed that you know how to weave in an end. Which is a crazy assumption given the many differences of opinion about how to accomplish that, or even when to accomplish it. Here are some methods, listed from easiest to most onerous.

Enclose ends in stitches as you go. As mentioned in Chapter 3, this method is a time-saver. If you are working along and have just created an end or two by adding a new color, lay those ends across the top of your work and work right over/around them, enclosing them in the base of your stitches for at least 2 in. or more. At that point, they will be sufficiently strapped in, and you can cut them close to the stitches you're working and keep going.

Hide them along the seam. If this end happens to be near an edge of a piece that's going to get sewed to another edge, eureka! You've just found your ideal place to hide the end. Thread the end into a tapestry needle, then run the needle down through the stitches at the edge of the piece for a few inches, then over a tiny bit on one stitch, then back up again in the other direction. Snip close to the piece.

Little rectangles, kinda sorta. Most methods described in a book or demonstrated in tutorials basically call for sewing the end into the finished work in a shape that turns out to be roughly rectangular. In other words, thread the end through a needle, then work it

Weaving the Fat Stuff

When working with a really bulky yarn, you might find it doesn't fit in your tapestry needle. That's all right. Split the strand into two or three, and thread one of the split pieces onto the needle, then weave in that piece. Repeat with the others. Sometimes this renders the yarn pretty fragile, so work gently.

down through an existing stitch, then across a row for a few inches, then down (or up) another stitch, then back across the row in the other direction. Actually, it really doesn't matter whether you make a rectangle shape or whether you go down first or across first. The important thing is to work your end in several directions for several inches, and both up and down, and to keep it hidden inside the stitches. If doing it the exact same way every time makes you feel secure, go for it. If some variety in the direction you sew lifts the monotony of the process, give that a go. Then cut the end close to your work and give the piece a gentle tug in several directions to make the cut end disappear into the work.

The extra-fancy way. Some crocheters do as the above, but as they're weaving with their tapestry needle, they take pains to split some of the crochet stitches with the needle here and there. Remember, the idea is to get the fibers in the end yarn to marry with the fibers in the

created piece, so the more surface-to-surface interaction, the better.

Just to be sure. Other crocheters enclose their ends inside stitches but do not snip the ends. They leave them dangling out of the work, and then use the tapestry needle to work these in. Double insurance.

And of course there are also people who knot, for extra piece of mind. Though crochet snobs may turn up their noses, nobody will arrest you for it, and as long as you can hide the knots among other stitches, what's the harm?

I've seen a friend weave in ends using only a crochet hook, not a tapestry needle. Is that kosher?
It can be done that way, but it's not as secure. Why? Because the hook is generally not able to lead the yarn through the fibers of the piece as intricately (or easily) as a needle can. The hook way is easier because you don't have to reach for a needle, but it is looser. Question to consider: How much wear and tear will this piece get? If it's an heirloom-quality afghan that will require a lot of laundering as various generations barf and pee on it, secure your ends with extra extra care. If it's an amigurumi monkey that's going to perch on your printer at work, hook weaving is fine.

My pattern says to weave in all the ends on my pieces before I assemble this sweater, but my crochet guru friend told me to always wait until the whole piece is done.
Your crochet guru friend has the right answer for her crochet guru self, and you need to figure out the right answer for you. A few factors: Will both sides of your work show? Because you can skip weaving in tails altogether if they're on the inside, say, of a tubular piece that will be stuffed and sewn up, so nobody can see the innards. Will the ends be hard to access once you've sewed

The Rock Star Way to Thread a Tapestry Needle

1. Lay yarn over needle.

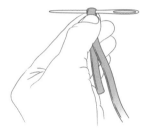

2. Pinch yarn in a tight fold over the needle.

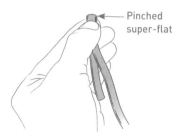

← Pinched super-flat

3. With your other hand, extract the needle, but hold the pinched yarn.

4. Now shove the eye right onto the pinched yarn. Pull the yarn through and you're done!

up the piece? That's why some patterns recommend weaving them in first. Lastly, what's psychologically better for you? Me, I like my pieces all neat and tidy and tail-free before I sew them together. But I know people who can't wait to see the item assembled in its finished shape, and find the weaving process much more tolerable after that, when they're so near the finish line.

Also, some people use long-enough tails in spots where they can sew with them, in which case it would be foolish to snip them off. Trial and error, baby. Whatever floats your boat.

This tutorial I watched says to weave in the ends at the "back" of my work. What if my work is meant to be viewed from both sides? Weaving on the back of the work is what you do if you've got a lot of colors going on and it's not feasible to weave only into the color that matches the end you are weaving. But most crochet work is thick enough that you can mostly weave from either side. If the yarn is the same color and you don't make any bumps or knots nobody will be able to tell.

In a couple of spots, I forgot to leave a long-enough end. Now I have these little 2-in. stumps of yarn sticking out, too short to weave it with a needle. Fixes?
This might not be the problem you think it is. If you are going to be sewing some kind of seam adjacent to the place where the end is hanging off, fold the stubby end along the seam and enclose it in the stitches when you make them. In other words, keep the stub in the center of any stitches you make with a needle, so the yarn wraps around and hides it. Or if you are crocheting a seam, keep that stub laid along the row you're crocheting, so it gets hidden as you go.

If neither of those are options, throw your whole piece right out the nearest window.

Kidding! Take your unthreaded tapestry needle instead, and weave it into some stitches near the stub, in and out (but not yet pulled through) a few times. At that point, thread your needle with the stub yarn, then pull through. Not threading before you insert the needle gives you some extra play. The truly fastidious among us won't be satisfied with this solution, however. We'll go back with a different length of yarn and weave through the area where the stub end is hidden, back and forth and up and down, just to keep it tucked in cozy, and then clip the ends of that extra yarn close to the piece, as if its ends were the original ones we were trying to hide. Some people also like to split the stub end into two strands and weave each half of it separately for extra security.

My crochet buddy's afghan came undone in the wash because she didn't secure the ends of it enough. I hate using a needle. Is there a no-needle safe method for granny squares?

There is, and for some reason it's fun, too. When you start a new color, leave about a 6-in. tail. Lay this tail over the area where you will work your first cluster of stitches. Eventually you get to the part where you need to bridge to the next cluster via chain stitches, so you'll have to do something different, right? When you're at the last double crochet in the cluster, wait until you have the last 2 loops of that stitch on your hook and then take the tail and flip it over (to the back of) the yarn you are about to finish the stitch with. Then finish the stitch. The tail is now intertwined with the last double crochet in the cluster.

Now flip the tail over the top of the working yarn and do your chain stitch (and flip it back again and do another chain if you are at a 2-chain space), and then when it is time to do your first double crochet of the next cluster, line up the tail with the working yarn and do the double crochet as if they are one piece of yarn, using them both for the yarn over. Then pull

Foundation Chain Tail: Erased!

If you think you can't get rid of that tail at the beginning of your chain stitch row until the very end of your project, think again. Complete the chain row and work back across it with your first row of stitches to the point just above the tail, which will be your last stitch in the first row. Then fold the tail up over the row before working the second row in the opposite direction, enclosing the tail in the bases of the stitches for several inches. Leave an inch or so of it dangling unenclosed at that point, and when you reach this dangle point coming back across the next row, lay the tail along your row of stitches again. Now you can enclose it going in the opposite direction. After a few inches, clip it close to the stitches. Tail? What tail?

that tail piece down to the base of the stitches, and do the next 2 double crochet in the cluster right over the tail end at the base. You can clip it here, or repeat from * for additional clusters if you want even more security.

THE INVISIBLE WAY TO END A CIRCLE

How picky are you? If you've got an eye for detail, you might notice that when you end a circle that's been worked in a spiral, even if you've done it neatly with a slip stitch, the ending point sticks out a little, causing a slight irregularity in the shape of the edge of the circle. Here's how to get rid of it.

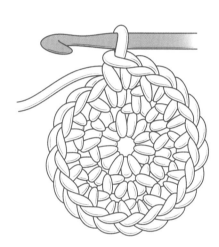

1. At the end of a spiral round, you could slip stitch to the next stitch to finish, but how about no.

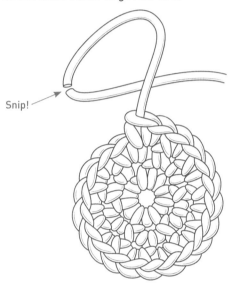

2. Instead, pull up the loop on the hook and cut it about 6 in. from the work.

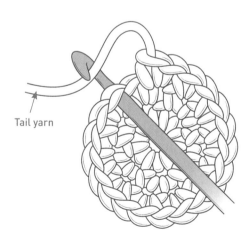

3. Skip one stitch, and then insert the hook under the next one. Pull the tail yarn through that stitch.

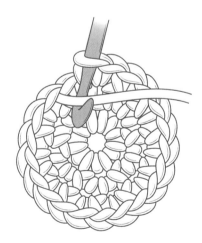

4. Insert the hook into the center of the last stitch from behind. Pull the tail through, then weave in the end.

Four Tips for Disaster-Free Sewing with Yarn

1. You don't need to put a knot in the end of the yarn, as you would if you were hand-sewing with thread. When pulling the needle through the crocheted pieces for the first time, simply refuse to pull it all the way through. Leave a couple inches not pulled through, then fold this end bit along the seam you're about to sew, and enclose it in your work. If you really prefer some kind of knot, consider this: Make a slipknot at the end of your yarn when you begin, dip your needle through your work, then thread it through the center of the slipknot and pull. You can fold the tail of the slipknot upward and enclose it in the stitches as you go.

2. Don't go nuts with length. About 18 in. of yarn is all you need at a time. You may want to use a really long piece of yarn, but yarn gets twisted and sometimes fuzzy as you work with it, so keep it to 18 in. or less.

3. In sewing, it's often nice to use a doubled-over thread, for extra strength. If you do that with yarn, you're going to get an Incredible Hulk of a seam. Almost always, single is better and way less prone to twisting and tangling.

4. If you've been working with a yarn that's at all bumpy or hard to frog, don't sew with that stuff. Pick a coordinated smoother yarn instead.

Getting Your Act Together

When it's time to sew one piece to another, patterns often stay pretty mum about how. So here's the lowdown:

Pins: The kind of straight pins you use in sewing are rarely good for temporarily holding pieces of crochet together when you're ready to sew stuff. That's because a piece of crocheted work is so much thicker than a piece of fabric, and the poor little straight pin can't deal. Instead, use safety pins, stitch markers, even bits of yarn that you tie. Line up the two sides that need to be joined flat on a table in front of you side by side, then put any of these little helpers in place every couple of inches or so. That'll keep your work from shifting as you go.

Sewing yarn: Again, 18 in. of whatever matches your work best.

Needle: Tapestry, naturally. Or upholstery. Really anything with a big-enough eye to fit the yarn.

Knot: (K)not necessary, really. But if you feel naked without one, try the slipknot method in the sidebar (above).

Technique: Well, it depends. A piece that has been crocheted tends to have a distinct top (the edge you worked last, which has little chain-stitch Vs across it), bottom (where the loops of the foundation chain are, if you used one), and sides (just the sides of the stitches, if worked in rows). So you may find yourself sewing two top edges together, or two side edges, or two bottom edges, or some combination of side and bottom. This can affect which stitch you choose. You also have to ask yourself what kind of seam you want. Does it need to be extra-sturdy, because it's holding something together that will get stressed a bunch (like the sides of a handbag)? Does it need to be invisible, so nobody notices there's a seam there? Or are you going for decorative? If you consider these factors, you can have an instant plan whenever you see the vague words "sew panels together" in a crochet pattern.

My eyes feel damaged after researching how to sew together crocheted pieces. So many methods! Tell me the basic ways, with no extra froufrou.

Yes! Keep in mind these are not the only answers, but they will work. Check out the chart on the facing page.

Simple, right? It makes sense if you think about it. Unlike with sewing, where material can't be attached edge to edge because it is too thin and will fray, crochet can be almost fused

Let's Split

"I got this idea after I discovered that the ends on one of the blankets I made were starting to wiggle out of the stitches I'd sewn them into. The blanket was one I'd made back in the early days, before I understood the best ways to weave in ends and the importance of making sure the ends are long enough to weave in properly. My daughter was younger then, and the blanket got quite a bit of rough handling, which meant I had quite a few bits that were poking out, but a lot of them were only a couple of inches long.

"So, to secure them firmly back into place and make sure they wouldn't go wandering again, I decided to split the short ends into two sections. Then I used a sharp yarn needle to weave in the two different bits. The first piece, I'd weave in to the right, making sure I doubled back on myself to secure it firmly, and I also used the sharp needle to make sure the end I was weaving got worked through the threads of the yarn of the other stitches, so it was harder for them to come out. Then I got the second piece and did the same, this time to the left. By doing it in opposite directions, the ends can't pop out as easily when the blanket is pulled about. It worked quite well, and those ends are still nicely tucked away."

—Sandra Paul

to another piece of crochet along its thicker side edge. Or it can be laid atop another piece, as in sewing with material. When you want an edge to disappear, use the mattress stitch. Your aim is to draw those edges together in such a way that the edges face each other and fuse, with the stitching that holds them together barely showing, if it's showing at all. When you lay a piece on top of another piece, you can either attach it with a running stitch or a whipstitch, which spirals around the sides of the work.

I used the running stitch to close the seams in a pocket, but small things (including my own fingers) keep poking out of it. What can I do about the gaps?
Try the backstitch instead, which is like a backward running stitch, but leaves fewer gaps. Here's how to do it. Needle comes up at 1, down at 2, up at 3, down at 4, etc. (see p. 69). This is definitely a more solid seam than a running stitch.

I crochet my seams together. I lay the pieces on top of each other and stick my hook in and pull up the yarn and single crochet, then repeat. Anybody got a problem with that?
The only problem is that it tends to make the seam bulky. The stitches create their own little ridge and so can be visible. Also, a hook does not dip into a piece of crochet as easily in some

spots as a needle can, so if you're attaching a double crochet edge to a single crochet edge, it's going to be trickier. But give it a try and see if it works. It is really nice to not have to deal with the needle sometimes.

Block Party

"Do I really have to?"

If that sentence conveys your attitude about blocking, you might want to skip this part. But don't! Don't skip this part, and don't skip blocking, either! Or at least, don't skip it without considering whether it will make a difference.

Blocking is the process of letting the stitches in your work get wet or steamy and then shaping them a bit before allowing them to dry. Truth be told, the fibers really enjoy this spa treatment. They reward you for it by getting all orderly, lining up just so. To the untrained eye, there might not be much difference, but trust the experts, there is a difference, and blocking is the best for uncurling edges. Deciding to skip blocking is kind of like deciding to skip the top coat after a manicure. Will anyone notice the missing extra layer of gloss? Maybe not. But if it's there, the whole thing looks better, and you know it.

There are times when blocking is pointless, though, and thus a waste of time. If you're working with a highly textured yarn where the stitches aren't that visible, forgetaboutit. If you've made something that's going to be stuffed, and so will hold its shape, like a little crocheted animal, skip blocking and make no apologies. The test is this: Will blocking improve my finished product if the stitches relax and look more regular? Usually the answer is yes, and with crocheted lace, the answer is way yes, but as a knitter also, I have to admit that I think blocking may be more important to the look of a plain knitted stitch

THE BASIC WAYS, BASICALLY

Pieces Attached	How to Do It
Edges attached side by side	Mattress stitch
Edges attached atop each other	Running stitch

Like a Surgeon

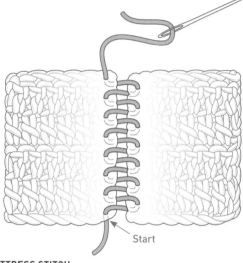

Start

MATTRESS STITCH
Start from the back (wrong side) with each stitch, pulling up through the front and alternating sides with each stitch.

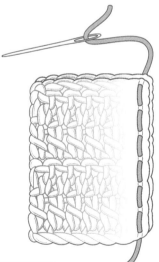

RUNNING STITCH
Up from behind, down through the front, up from behind close to that stitch, down through the front. Repeat!

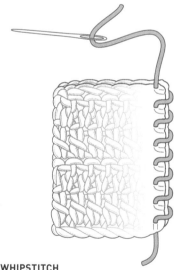

WHIPSTITCH
Up from behind, wrap around the edge, then up from behind again.

than a plain crochet stitch. In other words, again, don't let anyone boss you around. Try blocking; see if you like it. It really isn't that much of a pain, even for the impatient.

Hey, also: Be aware that blocking is something that some patterns call for, and others don't. But just because a pattern doesn't mention it doesn't mean it won't increase the cuteness of your work.

WET BLOCKING IN FIVE SIMPLE STEPS

1. Fill a container or sink with lukewarm water. Not hot! Are you insane? Just barely warm. Add a little (seriously, you don't need much) mild soap to it. Swish until you've got some suds, no biggie. By the way, right before step one is a good time to check the label on the yarn you used. Don't expose your work to anything the label suggests you avoid in the washing instructions.

2. Stick your work into the basin and squish it gently with your fingers until you think the water is pretty well soaked in. It is important to get all the fibers wet, even their innermost bellies, so let this puppy sit for at least 15 minutes, maybe giving it a gentle squish now and then. While you are waiting, grab a bunch of bath towels and some straight pins, maybe a cookie rack, maybe an electric fan, maybe a ruler. Refuse to answer questions from your family about what you are doing. It will make you seem mysterious.

3. Lift your work from the water and squish it a bit, with care, to get some water out. Then lay it in a lump on a towel while you fill up the sink with non-soapy water. It's time to rinse, so dunk your piece in the non-soapy water and repeat this rinsing step if you need to until all the soap seems to be gone. Nobody's going to keel over if some soap remains, by the way.

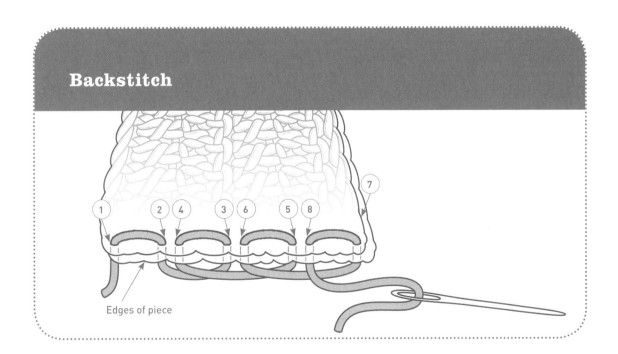

4. Set up a fluffy towel as your drying pad (you can leave it folded, as long as it's big enough to support your work spread out). To speed drying, you can put this drying pad over a cookie rack or any other structure that will allow air to circulate beneath it. Now squish the extra water from your work without wringing it in the slightest, lay it flat-ish on a different towel, and roll the towel up and smush on it with your hand, or even your feet or bottom, to take some of the water out of the work.

5. Finally, lay your work on the drying pad. Now use your skilled fingers to position the work into whatever shape you'd like it to take. Pin it down in this shape, with your pins not pushed totally into the towel. Summon your most critical gaze and assess whether this is the shape you desire. Use a ruler to check whether things are even if you want to be that way about it (totally optional). Set up the fan, and let the thing dry. When it is completely and totally 100 percent dry (no exceptions)—this could take days, or just a few hours, so test by feel—unpin and admire.

By the way, what would happen if you wore something before it was 100 percent dry? It would probably take the shape of your body or whatever curves it lies against. Sometimes this could be what you want, but usually it just results in distorted work.

Why is the soap necessary for blocking? It isn't. You can wet-block without soap. Soap is a nice extra step to clean the work, since you have been handling it like crazy, and maybe your yarn ball kissed the floor a few times.

What if my yarn is 100 percent acrylic? I heard blocking doesn't work on man-made yarns. There's debate about this. Some people say it doesn't work and in fact it will *ruin* your work,

Block That Block

Test of your common sense: What's the one time you should definitely not steam- or heat-block your work in any way? When it's dirty. Heat and steam set in stains as well as stitch patterns. So unless it's a really awesome stain in the shape of a bunny and you want to admire it forever, make sure you're working clean before you block.

and some say it does work and should be done. The only way to tell for your project is to test it with your particular yarn. Work up a little swatch if you're nervous, and try the steam method with that. Or use your gauge swatch. In fact, with some garments your pattern may tell you to block your gauge swatch before you start the project. This is actually quite smart if you are planning to block the final garment. Apples to apples, you know?

GETTING STEAMY

To block using the steam method—which is good for cotton yarns—pin your dry work to a towel in the desired shape, then let a steam iron hover over the work, and pat the steam in with your fingers (careful—steam can't help being insanely hot). Whatever you do, do not let the iron come in contact with the yarn if it is man-made or if the label indicates avoiding dryers/heat. Remember that some of this yarn

Killer Instincts

When heat comes too close to acrylic yarn, the yarn melts a bit (or a lot) and it's a bona fide disaster, right? That's why this type of mistake in knitting or crocheting is known as "killing" the yarn.

But there are times when you might want to kill your acrylic. And I don't just mean when you are sick of your project and don't care if someone flushes it down the toilet. "Killed" yarn becomes thinner, more limp, and smoother (kinda goes without saying, since it's partly melted). This can be the perfect solution when a project is too bulky or nubby, or too bunched up.

How to kill acrylic kindly? Set your iron on medium high heat and get a washcloth or small towel pretty wet. Lay out the piece you want to kill (let's just call it the victim) in the shape you want it to retain, then lay the wet washcloth on top of it. Double-check the positioning of the victim, because as many a tragic villain can tell you, killing is not reversible. You won't be able to frog any of your stitches after this, because they're going to be permanently melded. Now press the iron down onto the wet washcloth until it steams up a lot. Don't make an ironing motion back and forth; just lift and press in different sections over the part of the acrylic you want to kill. You may need to play a little with the heat and steam levels on the iron to get the effect you want. When your item is sufficiently flat and submissive, remove the washcloth and let the piece dry fully. Your floppy new friend is ready!

Caution: As with any type of killing, you'd better think about it first. Really and truly, test it with a crocheted swatch that uses the same stitches, same everything.

is basically plastic. You could end up with a ruined project and a gummed-up iron.

What if my yarn is super-fuzzy or delicate? In this case, especially if you're working with animal fibers like mohair, cashmere, silk, or alpaca, you can just lay out your work dry on a towel, pin it to the desired shape, spritz it wet with a spray bottle, then let it dry. What could be easier? This method is also good for acrylic if it's sensitive to the heat in steam. The spritz-and-dry is the best method when you're nervous about yarn damage. It's pretty dang safe.

I was about to block my garment, and now I'm noticing the pattern says to block each piece before putting it together. Do I need to undo my seams? Say no.
No. Just block the whole garment. If the pattern gives you a great reason for doing the blocking before assembly, consider that next time. But generally, you can block the whole critter.

In Case of Emergency . . . the Edge!

One beautiful feature of crochet is that you can work your stitches anywhere you please. Want to go across the row? Get to it. Around in a circle? Not a problem. Care to pick up stitches on a diagonal right down the center of a square you've just worked? Very well: Just dip in and pull up yarn with some slip stitches, and it's off to the races.

This wonderful flexibility can be your knight in shining armor when it comes to finishing your work. Whenever things are looking a little weird around the edges . . . hey, stick an edge on it! Crocheted borders can be like the tidy piping at the edge of upholstery, or they can be so gorgeous they steal the whole show.

A **single crochet** stitch is often the easiest way to give your piece some structure and a neater outer edge. Put a slipknot on the yarn you want to edge with, stick your hook into the stitch at the edge where you'd like to begin, then place the slipknot on the hook, pull that slipknot loop through the work, and make your first crochet stitch. After you've done a few stitches, examine your work. A single crochet stitch looks different from the front and back; if you think the side of the stitch facing the back of your work looks better than the side you're working with, pull out your work and start again, working on the other side of the work this time (if it's worked in rows) or in the other direction (if it's a circle).

Another reliable option for edging is a **reverse single crochet**, also known as a crab stitch. It looks like a twisted rope at the edge of your work and is so easy. Attach the edging yarn to your work with a slipknot, then slip-stitch in the last stitch in your row or round, chain 1 in that last stitch, then insert your hook, from front to back, through the same stitch the chain 1 is worked in. Yarn over, and pull that loop through the stitch to the front of the work. You'll have 2 loops on your hook. Then yarn over again and pull that yarn through both loops on the hook. Repeat this with the stitch before that, so you are working backward along the row: Insert the hook front to back, yarn over, and pull that loop through (2 stitches on the hook, looking a little twisted when your hook is held parallel to the edge of the row you're working), yarn over again, and pull through. That's all there is to it. It feels really weird to be working backward at first, but you'll get the hang.

To get a little frilly, you can also try a **picot**, which is a fun word to say. There are quite a few variations on the picot, but one to try is to attach your edging yarn via slipknot and slipstitch in the first stitch in row or round, then chain 3, work 1 single crochet in the first chain, skip 1 stitch, then work a single crochet in the next stitch in the row. Repeat from *.

For single crochet you work an edge stitch in every other row, and for double crochet you work a stitch in every row. True?
Not necessarily. It's a good guideline, but with edges you can't really follow a formula. It depends on what hook you use, how tight your stitches are, etc. So use your own best judgment when working around the sides of pieces. The only rule of thumb in edging that generally holds is to add extra stitches, as in 2 or 3 total, in the corners of a piece so they lie flat.

Before I added the edging, my piece was lying pretty flat. Now it's curling up. Diagnosis?
Probably, you did not use enough stitches around the edge. Try using more. Of course, if you use too many, your piece also won't lie flat. It will ripple. Experiment to find the right number, watching your stitches closely as you go. The edging stitches should look just as flat as the stitches in the piece. If they start to curl up, frog a bit and add more.

Cleans Up Nicely

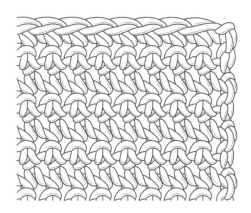

PLAIN OL' SINGLE CROCHETS

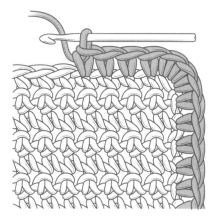

EDGED IN STYLE WITH SC BORDER

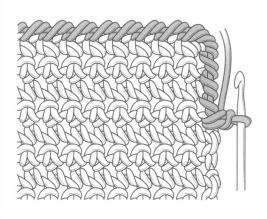

REVERSE SC BORDER

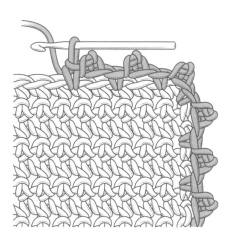

PICOT BORDER

Assorted Finishing Emergencies

I'm working on a stuffed crocheted brown bear, and now that I've stuffed him, I can see his white stuffing through the stitches. Why did this happen?

Crochet stitches do have a little space between them, and stuffing can show through. Anesthetize your bear, remove that fiberfill stuffing you probably used, and stuff him instead with the same yarn you made him out of, or at least a yarn that matches his outsides better. When he comes to, he'll be grateful and feel a lot less exposed.

My favorite wool scarf got into a load of washing, and now it's noticeably smaller! Is it no longer my favorite wool scarf, or is there a remedy?

Because it is wool, you can try to reblock it . . . unless it went in the dryer. If it went in the dryer, it is pretty much toast, but I've been known to try to reblock those, too (with limited success—the scarf never looked like its original airy self again, but could still be used). Follow all the regular steps for wet blocking, but this time, try some fabric softener or hair conditioner in the soaking water before you rinse.

I crocheted a baby blanket, but now I am noticing that it's embarrassingly scratchy—my punishment for using cheap yarn. Is it possible to soften this stuff up?

Potentially. Some acrylic yarns really love to be put through a wash cycle in your machine and (though we hesitate to type this, because we are mostly allergic to the concept of the dryer when it comes to things we have made with our hands out of yarn) a run through the dryer also. Obviously, this is a case where you should crochet up several swatches and test

them before subjecting your project to the same treatment. Some crocheters swear by a fabric softener rinse, a fabric softener sheet in the dryer, vinegar used in place of detergent, or a hair conditioner soak before rinsing. Some even machine-wash and -dry their skeins of yarn in a closed lingerie bag before beginning a project. Since not all acrylic yarns act the same, it wouldn't make sense to recommend a specific treatment here. Experiment away, and see what you find. And by the way, lots of classy crocheters use cheap yarn now and then. It serves a purpose.

I knitted a handbag out of a cotton yarn and was so pleased with it . . . until it started to stretch. I think I've gained several inches in strap length. What gives?

What gives is the cotton fibers themselves. They do tend to stretch when worn (just like your jeans). Next time you make something with cotton, try the steam block on your gauge swatch and on the finished item. That should lock the size in place. For this project, you might have to unsew the strap and shorten it by removing rows, if that's possible. Or, much easier fix, stuff the bag portion of your project with a light-colored fabric to retain its shape, then wash and dry the bag, checking it in the dryer often so it doesn't shrink too much. Naturally, you should check the yarn label before doing this, to be sure that the yarn is allowed in your appliances.

I wore my crocheted shrug one time—once!—and it got all pilly under the arms, with little fuzzy tufts on the shoulder. How can I cope?

Abrasion is the culprit. You can probably avoid the shoulder tufts if you wear this shrug with nothing rubbing against it—no handbag, no winter coat—even place your seatbelt carefully. But the pilly underarms you're kinda stuck with. Except you're not, because you can shave them off. That's right: with a disposable razor. Pretend they're legs. Or you can buy an electronic de-pilling shaver, which is fun to use, or you can trim the pills off with scissors. There are also pill-removing stones (similar to pumice stones) and combs. The one thing you should not do is yank at the pills with your fingers. That beats the fiber up, damaging your hard work.

I did everything I was supposed to, but . . . I just don't like this sweater on me. And I feel like I have to wear it, because I made it. Is that nuts?

Not nuts, but a little too general. What don't you like about the sweater? Maybe it needs to be blocked for better drape. Maybe it needs an edging. Maybe it's itchy, and you'd be okay wearing a T-shirt under it. Maybe the shape is all right everywhere but the shoulders, where it's really wrong. Put the piece aside for a couple of days while your disappointment dies down, and then try it on again. Wear it to a local yarn shop and ask for a second opinion. Minor adjustments that might not occur to you may help you make friends with this garment again. If not, donate it to someone else and move on. Life's too short

to dwell on less-than-thrilling projects! But it's great if we can learn from them.

Also, please don't take it as a sign of poor workmanship if a pattern that looked great in a photo on a model does not look good on you. Think of how many times you've thought something on a hanger in a store would suit you, and then you get in the dressing room and learn how wrong you were. Was the garment you tried on hideously flawed? No. You liked it at first sight. It just wasn't good for your build or coloring. So be kind to your crafting self. And maybe next time you pick up your yarn and a hook, try something less specific to body type, such as a scarf or handbag or hat.

I just did all the finishing work for this scarf for a friend, and I admire it too much to part with it. I mean, seriously: I'm gazing at it lovingly like every 20 minutes. Have I gone off the deep end?

That's called crochet love and yes, you have gone off the deep end. But it's a good thing. Keep that scarf, and make your friend one just like it. When a project goes right, it isn't a sign of low intelligence to wallow in the joy.

Are You a Good Glitch or a Bad Glitch?

Sometimes, when you make a crochet mistake, you notice it as it happens. Other times, though, you might be so caught up in your project's journey from its ugly stage to cuteness that you don't see the error of your ways until your project is almost done, and then you must choose: frog or fudge? Often you'll have to frog, but many times you can rescue your project so deftly that you might end up prouder of the first aid than of the item itself. This chapter is for those instances.

Edging Errors

I lost a stitch occasionally at the end of a row on this baby blanket, then made up for it with increases. Now some rows are shorter than others. Can I still fix this?

In most cases you can. Your magic treatment? Add a secret border! This is not like adding the official border as described in Chapter 4. A secret border is a border worked in the same color yarn (when possible) as the rows it touches, so that this border seems to be an extension of the piece. Then, if you choose, a decorative border, in whatever color yarn you select, can be worked around the secret border. Here's the fudge, though: During the crocheting of the secret border, when you get to the edges of the rows that seem short, instead of putting a single crochet in that spot, work a half-double crochet, or an extended single crochet (explanation on p. 78) to bring up the height of that area. For extra camouflage, make the final (official) border something with wavy edges, such as a scalloped edge (see p. 79) or a simple picot. This will keep the eye moving enough that it won't think to go to the places where you once saw flaws.

What if I have uneven edges to hide, but I don't want to add a border? Is there a way to graft in a stitch here and there at the edges?

Oooh, desperate question. But yes! Crochet is flexible that way. Let's say you're working a bunch of rows of double crochet, but on one row you got confused and left a stitch off the end. And then, not wanting to frog, on the next row you corrected it by adding an extra stitch. It didn't seem like it would be a biggie, but now it's bothering you. The solution: Fill in the missing stitch by dipping your hook into the stitch below the missing one, chaining 2, then using a 3rd chain to attach to the row above.

The Secret Border

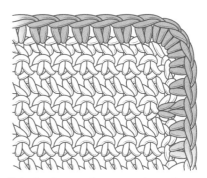

If the border was the same color as the swatch, would you be able to spot the short row?

There is a missing stitch here, so when working the border, disguise it using an elevated single crochet, or a double crochet in that spot.

The Shameless Graft

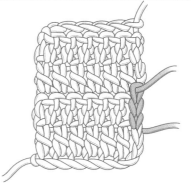

To disguise a missing stitch, just attach yarn, chain 2, and attach it again at the top of the stitch. Then weave in the ends, and nobody will know!

Single Crochet in Stilettos: The Extended Single Crochet

This crochet stitch is no spotlight seeker. Indeed, it's a tad obscure. Most crocheters probably don't know it exists, and few patterns call for it. But it's handy to have in your bag of fudging tricks because it does stand a little taller than a single crochet stitch, but lacks the column-like bulk of a half-double crochet. Here's how to do it.

Dip your hook into the stitch as if to do a single crochet, yarn over, and pull the yarn through the stitch (again, just like single crochet). Now you have 2 loops on your hook. Yarn over and pull through just the loop on the hook that's closest to the tip of the hook (the first loop), so you again have 2 loops on your hook. Yarn over and pull through both loops on the hook. See? It's kinda pretty, and should get out more often.

It wouldn't be kosher, but sometimes when I realize that I've accidentally added a stitch in one row, I'm tempted to simply skip a stitch in the next. Would that make up for it?

Yes, in many cases it would fix your stitch count problem. But it might leave a noticeable hole. The better option is to decrease by crocheting 2 stitches together. Not that you'd ever do that (wink, wink). If you are working a series of stitches that form a pattern, though, it's usually better just to suck it up and frog. Only do the decrease option if it's not going to ruin the order of what comes after it. Experiment and see.

I am hating how holey this latest scarf is. I wanted it to be warm, but air comes whoosh-ing right through. Should I sew up all the gaps between stitches?

Sewing up a hole is perfectly okay at any point. But you may get overwhelmed trying to do that for a whole scarf. This is an instance in which you might like instead to line the underside of the scarf with something that feels good against the skin—silk, or satin, or even felt or fleece or velvet. Elvis reportedly started wearing his amazing jumpsuits to conceal his midsection and poke fun at himself; Michael Jackson may have started wearing his sparkly gloves to hide some discoloration on his hands. Prince's sweet heels? He's tiny. Take your supposed flaw and work some style around it. You may start a trend.

I can't believe it, but while I was cutting a woven-in end close to my work, I cut through a stitch. Now my whole project is going to unravel, right?

In the rare event that you cut right through a stitch, freeze. Then set your piece of work gently aside, leaving some marker near the spot so you won't lose it, and forbid anyone in the vicinity to stress that spot in any way. If you are working with a woolly or fuzzy fiber, cutting through a stitch is actually no big deal. Thread a needle with some of the same fiber, stab it into an area a few inches from the stitch, weave it back and forth through your work in a few directions to stabilize it, then run some of that yarn right along the path of the broken stitch, copying the shape of the surrounding stitches. Then weave the yarn into your work near the other edge of the cut stitch. Trim ends, and you should be fine.

If this cut stitch is in a slippery, non-grippy yarn or thread, you need to take extra action, such as using a washable fabric glue (i.e., one that does not dissolve when washed) to stabilize the area. Keep the glued portion as small as you possibly can: Your aim is to rejoin the fibers where they were supposed to be joined. When this has dried, try weaving some extra yarn/thread through this zone as described above, to reinforce.

In worst-case scenarios, where your stitched or glued fix screams "blunder!" to all who gaze upon the crocheted item, this spot may now be a great candidate for some distracting adornment, such as a button, a pom-pom, or a crocheted flower. What started out as a disaster may end up being your favorite part of the piece. Hey, at least it has a story!

I finished a cute amigurumi mouse, but it looks wrong. A friend told me I made it inside out. How can I tell?
When you work back and forth in rows, the back and the front of a piece of crochet looks basically the same. But when working in rounds, as in *amigurumi* (the Japanese word for adorable little crocheted creatures), one side of the work looks pretty different from the other. The preferred outside is the one where no dashes are visible on the stitches.

A Go-To Concealing Border

If you're looking for a nice, wavy decorative border to stick on work that's a little wavy itself, try the scalloped edge, which comes out looking like the curvy edges of an old-fashioned portrait frame. Attach yarn via a slipknot or just via pulling up a loop somewhere along the edge of your work or your secret border (not in a corner of it), *work a single crochet, skip 2 stitches, work 5 double crochet into the next stitch, skip 2 stitches again, single crochet 1 stitch, then repeat from * around the remainder of the piece. When you come to a corner, center the cluster of double crochets there, and instead of double crocheting 5, work 8 into that spot. To plan out exactly how many scallops to put on the side of your piece, you can work one and measure it and do some math to see how many fit. Or you can eyeball it all the way around. The great thing about the scallops is that you can use the full 7-stitch span to work one, or you can pull the span in or stretch it out a little if that works better for fitting the length of the edge you're working on.

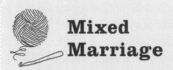

Mixed Marriage

To sew a lining into a crocheted piece—or really to attach fabric to crochet of any kind—you can either sew by hand with sewing thread and a sewing needle, or use a sewing machine. Punch little holes in your fabric where you want the stitches to go (mark them carefully first!), using a tiny hole punch, awl, or even electric drill, and then crochet into these holes, securing both layers together.

However, it's entirely up to you to decide which side is right and which one is wrong. Sometimes the "wrong" side might actually look better to you. It's not a federal law.

My amigurumi has weird gaps in it. I'll sew them up, whatever. But how can I avoid them next time?

If the gaps are all over the piece, your best bet is to fill the amigurumi with yarn in the same color as the work, instead of with fiberfill, as mentioned in Chapter 4. But if it's just in a few spots, here's a technique tweak to consider: Are you using an invisible increase and decrease?

To increase "invisibly" (it's not invisible, but it's less visible), work 2 stitches in the front loop/arm only of the V at the top of the stitch you're working into. This cuts down on the bulk of the increase. Invisible decreases are even

sneakier: Insert your hook into the front loop only of the next stitch, then the front loop only of the stitch after that (you may need to twist your hook as you work to make this easier). Then yarn over and pull through the first 2 loops on the hook, then yarn over and pull through the final 2 loops. Alternatively, some people invisible-decrease by putting the hook into the front loops only of the next 2 stitches, then yarn over and pull through all 3 loops on the hook. Try these methods and see which you like best. It's kind of a tie, but they all make for smoother changes than the usual both-loops increases and decreases.

I made a scarf composed of crocheted circles joined together. But they curled up like taco shells after I finished them. Am I stuck with tacos? I worked with acrylic.

You can try to block acrylic, of course, even though that doesn't always work. But since a scarf gets twisted around so much, even successful blocking probably isn't going to help a ton. Another solution would be to back the circles with a layer of interfacing (for sewing) under a layer of decorative fabric, such as fleece. Just make sure whatever you use for interfacing and decorative fabric is washable and won't bleed its color onto your scarf. Felt might be tempting, but it isn't famous for washing well.

Dealing with Misfits

I made my love a basic crocheted winter hat, and it's waaaay too baggy on him. Is there a way to tighten up the hat, or do I need a fatter-headed boyfriend?

There's hope. If this is a hat that was worked as a flat piece of crochet and then gathered at the top to form the hat shape, you probably know what to do: Carefully undo the side seam, then frog several rows of the hat. Pin as if there's

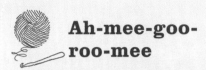

Ah-mee-goo-roo-mee

How does one even pronounce *amigurumi*? It's ah-mee-goo-roo-mee. But some people say ah-me-guh-rum-ee, no tragedy. It's Japanese for knitted/crocheted stuffed toy. Say it quickly and hold up your incredibly cute knitted/crocheted stuffed toy and nobody will question whether you're saying it right.

but make sure you check on the item periodically and also check that these actions won't destroy/melt your yarn (check the yarn's label, in other words).

A third option is a little time-consuming, but can work great. Buy some elasticized thread and, beginning at the crown of the hat, sew this thread through the hat in a spiral pattern, working downward, from top to brim. Make sure the elastic is concealed inside the yarn, closer to the inside of the hat than the outside, and check your tension now and then by trying the hat on the model. Secure the thread at the brim of the hat with several backstitches and a knot, because you want it secure. If that baby blows, it's fat-hat city all over again.

Alternatively, you could just have your guy grow his hair out until it's puffy enough to fill the mega-hat. Yeah, good luck with that one.

I have the opposite problem: a hat that's too small for my own head. How can I stretch it? You can do the opposite of almost all of the tactics in the previous answer. If you can take the hat apart partly and add extra rows to a side seam or to the bottom, now's your chance. Or get it wet (or use any of the blocking

a new seam, and try it on your man's noggin. Repeat until you've got the right fit, then sew it up all official.

If this is a piece worked in the round from the top down, try it on him and pay attention to where it gets too big. It may be that you can frog just part of it and re-crochet it with fewer increases if worked from the top down, or more decreases if worked from the brim up.

But let's say you really have zero desire to mess with your stitches. You can try to shrink the hat, but this may shrink it in all dimensions if you're not careful. Natural fibers are happy to shrink, whereas acrylic can be impossible, or can take maximum effort. Soak the hat in warm water and swish it around in the water with tongs or your hand. Watching carefully to be sure you don't overshrink, rescue the item when it seems a bit smaller. Then gently squeeze excess water from it and lay it out flat to dry in the desired shape and size. Hotter water and a clothes dryer can amplify the shrinking process if the above doesn't work,

Keepin' It Tight

Here's another amigurumi idea: When you choose your yarn, check the yarn label to see what hook size is recommended, and then go a size smaller. Maybe even two.

And Speaking of Sewing Things Up . . .

When researching this book, I was delighted to speak with Edie Eckman, author of so many amazing crochet books, including *The Crochet Answer Book*, *Around the Corner Crochet Borders*, and *Beyond the Square Crochet Motifs*. Guess what the single tip she wanted to share with readers was? To leave a long-enough length of yarn dangling.

"When adding new yarn, don't skimp on the ends," she advises. "Leave a long-enough tail of both the old yarn and the new yarn to weave in securely. Depending on the yarn you are using, that means leaving anywhere from 4-in. to 6-in. tails."

It's tempting sometimes to make the tails shorter and crochet right over them. If you're confident that's going to work, more power to you. But having a little extra yarn hanging there is never a bad idea. The aim is to give yourself elbow room to finish your work in a way that never looks like anyone sweated over finishing your work.

methods approved for your fiber type) and see how much you can stretch that sucker. Sometimes soaking it in hair conditioner can soften up the fibers enough to help them relax and stretch. At a beauty supply store, you can buy a foam wig stand/head form, which is great for stretching a wet hat over. Pin it in place with sewing pins, then let it dry. You can also use any rounded object, such as a foam ball or even a watermelon to shape a drying hat (when your family asks what the heck is going on with that watermelon, just give them an evil glare). The exception, of course, is a felted hat. It's not getting any bigger, sorry. Give it to some bald-headed doll or baby and move on with your life.

I crocheted a sweater and it looks dumb on me, all baggy in the bust. I followed the pattern for my size exactly, I just know it. Why this curse? Sweaters are hard to fit, which is why some of us avoid making them. But crucial to making them work with your bod is making sure you don't just measure your torso around in a circle, but measure your front from armpit to armpit, and your back and bust the same way. If the sweater is made in two pieces, in other words, your measurements should be considered that way, too. Obviously, some people have a big bust, which needs extra material in the front piece, but does not need extra material in the back. Others lack the assumed bustular dimensions and end up with too much nonsense going on in the finished armpits as a result. Sizing patterns is kind of an advanced skill, but understanding this basic notion about measuring can go a long way toward making you comfortable.

The best way to fix a crocheted sweater that's baggy in the bust is to take it apart at the side seams and narrow that area, either by sewing deeper seams (try pinning it first), or frogging, though that may not work for the pattern you're using. Remember that even though someone else wrote the pattern for this garment and considers it sacred, it's your garment now, and you can do to it whatever you like. For rule followers, this can be a tough one to swallow, but it's true.

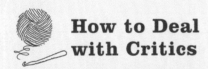

How to Deal with Critics

When an observer—especially one you love—makes a critical comment about something you've made, take a deep breath. Then recite this useful phrase: "Well, I'm learning." As you walk away, considering the comment and taking from it what you can, remind yourself how far you've come—and also how much your critical loved one had better shape up if he or she wants to receive the awesome things you will someday be making effortlessly.

Further Adventures in Hooking: A Toolbox for Cuteifying

Smart crocheters know things can, and will, go wrong. That's why it's good to have a few basic wow-things-are-going-so-right crochet moves mastered. Below are some favorites.

THE PUFF STITCH FLOWER

The Puff Stitch Flower is like the cutest crocheted flower ever. Some people use it to make whole blankets, like a carpet of connected flowers, very pretty (if a little stiff and thick for a blanket). It also makes a handy adornment. If you crochet a simple pair of wrist warmers, like the ones on p. 91, then stick a few of these on them— not so simple anymore. Same goes for hats. They're also good for headbands, necklaces, and decorating ribbons on packages. Gotta have Puffy in your bag of tricks.

Some people do it with double crochets in the first round, which makes a bigger center, or with no crochets in the first round (working petals into the magic ring), which results in a flower with no center—just big, fat, touch-me petals. All are super-cool, and accomplished so quickly you get a neat little thrill.

The Puffy Lil' Flower

HOW TO MAKE IT

You can use any yarn and any hook. Use the same color for the whole flower, or one color for the center of the flower and another for the petals, or a different color for every dang petal if you feel inspired.

Flower Center

Ch 4 and sl st to form a loop (or, much better in this case because it gets tight, make a magic loop/ring as described on pp. 56–57). Sc 11 into loop. Join round with sl st (11 sts in round).

1st Petal

Ch 3. Yarn over (yo) and insert hook into same st those 3 chs are extending out of. ***Yo and pull up through st to same height as 1st ch-3 in round. Yo and insert hook into same st, yo and pull up through st to same height as previous sts**. Repeat from *. Then yo and insert hook into next st in round. Repeat from * (just instructions in bold) 2 times. You now have a bunch of loops on your hook. Yo one more time and—pressing the hook up against the inside of the tops of these loops to make it easier—pull that yarn all the way through the loops and through the top ch in the ch-3 at the beginning of the petal. Ch 2. Join with sl st to next st in round.

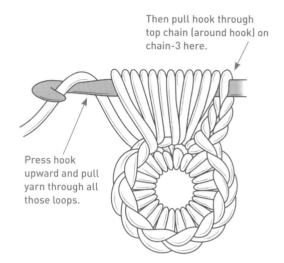

Then pull hook through top chain (around hook) on chain-3 here.

Press hook upward and pull yarn through all those loops.

2nd through 6th Petals

Work as for 1st petal. After 6th petal, secure with sl st to final st in round. Break off yarn and weave in ends.

BLOOMING ROSE

Roses, like puffy flowers, really shine in crochet. They bloom gorgeously off the hook and look pretty when stuck on just about everything. You can even make a quick tube of ribbed crochet for your wrist, then sew a few of these in different sizes on there for your own permanent corsage. Of the many variations one can do, here is a lovely quick one. You build it flat first, then roll it up like a sleeping bag to bring it to life.

A Really Good Rose

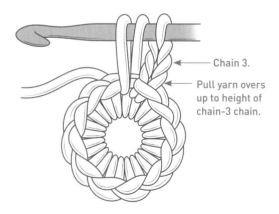

Chain 3.

Pull yarn overs up to height of chain-3 chain.

HOW TO MAKE IT

Any size hook and yarn will work. It depends on what size you want your rose to be.

Ch 21.

Row 1: In 5th ch from hook (dc, ch 2, dc), ch 2, sk 2 chs, (dc, ch 2, dc) in next ch. Repeat this pattern across row until 1 ch remains. Dc in final ch.

Row 2: Ch 3, turn, in 1st ch-2 space, then skip the next ch-2 space. Repeat from * across row. Atop last dc, work 1 dc.

Row 3: Turn, work 9 dc in next ch-2 space, sc in next ch space, repeat from * across row. Sl st to final ch-2 space. Break off yarn but leave a long tail.

FINISHING

Working from side without tail you just cut, roll the rose up with final row at top, coiling the rose until it looks . . . like a rose. Thread tail onto tapestry needle, and when you've got the rose tweaked the way you want it, sew up through its layers and then down again to secure the rose in its finished shape. Weave in ends.

AMAZEBALLS

If you get a handle on the basic ball shape in crochet, you can create amigurumi (as most are based on this shape), decorative cherries, buttons, centers of flowers, noses, holiday ornaments, hacky sack balls, you name it. Knowing how to make a half-ball, or dome, also comes in super-handy. As with the flowers above, you can vary the size by varying the yarn and hook size.

Amazeballs

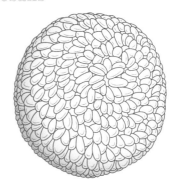

HOW TO MAKE IT

Ch 4 and sl st to form loop. Or use magic loop.

Round 1: Sc 6 into loop, join with sl st to form circle (6 sts in round). Place marker in last st of round.

Round 2: Sc 2 into each of the 6 sts in previous round (12 sts). Move marker up to last st of this round.

Round 3: *Sc 2 in 1st st, sc, sc 2 in next st, and repeat from * around round (18 sts). Move marker up to last st in round.

Round 4: *Sc 2 in 1st st, sc in next 2 sts, sc 2 in next st, and repeat from * around round (24 sts). Move marker up to last st in round.

Rounds 5–9: Work sc in each st around round (24 sts). Move marker up at end of each round.

Round 10: *Sc2tog (using front loops only for all decreases in this pattern, if you prefer the invisible decrease), sc 2, sc2tog. Repeat from * to end of round (18 sts). Move marker up to last st.

Round 11: *Sc2tog, sc, sc2tog. Repeat from * to end of round (12 sts). Move marker up to last st.

Round 12: *Sc2 tog in each st of round (6 sts). Stuff ball with fiber fill or scrap yarn in a similar color. Remove marker and fasten off last st, leaving a long tail. Weave tail in and out through the 6 sts in this round and pull tightly. Weave in end/tail.

EMERGENCY FUR

The loop stitch is a simple variation on a single crochet stitch—but a thousand times more fun-looking. It yields a texture that's either a lawn of loop, or a furlike shag of cut strands of yarn sticking up, and it's perfect for creating hair on dolls and also for trimming sleeves and collars of projects as if it were fur. Use it as a great distraction accent for a piece that may have a few flaws elsewhere, or as a finishing touch on some of your best work. Yeah, but watch out. When some of us started doing this stitch, we ended up so into it we started crocheting rugs.

Emergency Fur

HOW TO MAKE IT

Step 1: Using any yarn and the corresponding hook size, chain a row of desired length, then work 1 row of sc. For the 2nd row, begin making a sc st by inserting the hook into the st, but pull up the yarn in a triangle as shown.

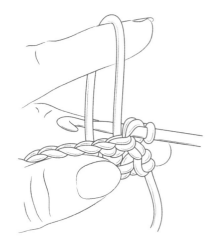

Hold yarn like this and pull both strands through the stitch. This creates the loop.

Step 2: Pull the 2 strands of yarn at the bottom of the triangle through the st (after which 3 loops will be on your hook), and finally yo and pull that yarn through the 3 loops on your hook. Repeat this for every st across the row. When you're done with your loop stitch area, you can decide whether you like the loopy look or whether you want to cut the loops.

Note: Naturally, if you're working in rows, you have to work the loop stitch every other row, unless the effect you're looking for is loops coming off both the front and the back of your work. But every other row is just fine: It still means plenty of loops per square inch. Want more? Then work in the round. That way, you can work every single stitch as a loop stitch, and get the thickest fake fur possible.

HOW TO DO THE BASIC TUNISIAN CROCHET STITCH

There's such joy in trying something new. If you've hit the wall with any stage of crochet, that's a great time to put away the problematic work and develop an additional skill, just for fun. Tunisian crochet sounds so exotic and fancy, but it's really pretty simple. This is the basic stitch, but there are others you can learn, too. Here's how:

Step 1: Get your Tunisian crochet hook, which, as mentioned in Chapter 1, looks like a hybrid crochet hook and knitting needle: a really long hook with a stopper on the end. Use it to ch 20.

Step 2: In 2nd ch from hook, insert hook into back hump of the ch st, yo, and pull that yarn through. Now you have 2 loops on your hook.

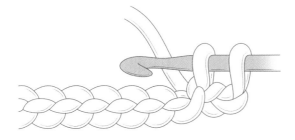

Step 3: Repeat this for all the other back humps of the ch sts. At the end of the row, you will have 20 loops on your hook. See why it has to be a long hook?

The Teeny Weeny Sweater

The first time I designed a crocheted sleeveless sweater (in junior high school) I was so thrilled with myself—until I sewed up the side seams and tried it on. Suddenly it was a corset—way too small. Trying to get it off came within inches of triggering my claustrophobia. But then I discovered something that has helped me understand other crochet patterns: It's possible to make a tiny sweater fit by taking it apart again at the side seams, crocheting an extra rectangle of sweater that runs from bottom edge to armpit, and grafting that in. When I did this on both sides, the sweater magically fit. In retrospect, it was still a devastatingly hideous sweater nobody ever should have worn. But at the time I was so glad I'd found a way to make it fit without having to redo my existing work. Notice how I'm not posting a photo. No observers were ever inspired to take one.

Step 4: That last step was not much fun, but don't worry, it gets better. In Tunisian crochet, you do not flip your work when you go back and forth across rows. It always faces you. So the next step is to yo and pull through just the first loop. Then work the rest of the row by yarning over and pulling through 2 loops at a time, until there is just 1 loop left on the hook. You have finished your foundation row. **Note:** For this step, I, usually a pencil-grip crocheter, switch to the knife-hold style. Just seems easier.

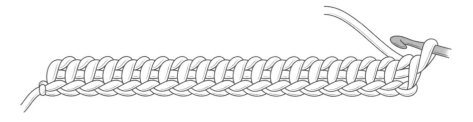

Step 5: Next, you will be working into the vertical pieces of yarn that you see in the foundation row. Here's what they look like:

Step 6: Insert hook into 2nd vertical, yo, and pull up loop. Continue across row like this, remembering to do final vertical. You should have 20 loops on your hook.

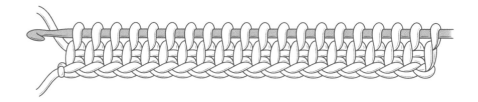

Step 7: For the next "row," which is really considered the second part of a 2-row row in Tunisian crochet, repeat the step at the top of this page. That is considered the end of Row 1.

Step 8: Repeat these last 2 steps as many times as you like. And there you have it, you're off to the races, Tunisian-style.

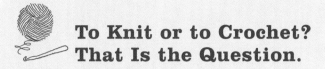

To Knit or to Crochet?
That Is the Question.

After drooling over a handmade capelet in a store a few years back, I bought it so I could copy it in a different color. The catch: It was knitted, and I wasn't in a two-needle mood. No problem, I thought. I know how to make that shape in crochet as well as in knitting. I'll just match the yarn type.

Three rows into this project, I realized my folly. The capelet's appeal depended on its measured bulk, but each crocheted stitch is generally about twice as chunky—using significantly more yarn—than a knitting stitch. Not only was I going to run out of yarn if I kept going, I was going to make something so thick I'd essentially be wearing a doormat on my back. Fashion fail.

As much as they get confused with each other by non-crafters, knitting and crochet are not equivalent. If you know how to do both, you've got a little dilemma on your hands. Should you knit it, or go the crochet way?

The Devil in the Details
Because crochet stitches tend to be thicker, crochet is your best bet when you want something to have a good structure to it, and knitting is preferable when you're seeking drape. By adjusting your yarn choice—say picking thinner yarn for crochet, or choosing a thicker yarn for knitting when you crave more structure—you can make allowances for this. But it's a good general principle to consider.

Knitting and crochet have different flavors and connotations. Because we humans are so accustomed to seeing machine-made knitting, knitted items have a more classic and manufactured look. Knitting looks more traditional. Crocheting rocks a bit of a funky 1970s vibe, since people still associate it with afghans worked in oranges and greens and browns. You could see this as a negative, but honestly, this association can make crocheted work more playful and tongue-in-check. Maybe that's what you want: Something that broadcasts its hand-madeness a hair more strongly than knitting does.

I like to remember that a project doesn't have to be exclusively knitted or crocheted. You can knit the body of a bag, then crochet its strap. Or knit the dome of a winter hat, then crochet a ticker edging for structure on the brow. I once saw a beautiful handmade scarf that alternated patches of knitting and patches of crochet. It was worked in only one oatmeal color, but had such a fascinating variety of texture. I'm glad its maker didn't feel limited by medium. Two tricks in the bag are sometimes better than one.

Six Sweet Designs to Conquer

Bad things may happen to good crocheters, granted, but not in this chapter! Good things here. Only good things. These six patterns have been thoughtfully designed, offering you simple access to finished projects so cute you'd buy them if you saw them in a store. They're also super-pleasing to crochet, each step of the way. None of them requires a crazy investment of time, so chances are you'll finish them—with pride and flair and (because you've got the other five chapters handy) expertise to spare. If you're like me, you'll end up wanting to work another one in the same pattern, different colors, immediately after you've woven in the last end. Enjoy!

Eve's Rib Wrist Warmers

What's that thing they say about crochet? That it's kinda stiff, that it's not as good as knitting at making stretchy tubes? Nonsense. The secret to getting a nice pliant tube shape is working in one loop of the V-shape at the top of crochet stitches. And as you can see here, the results are so knitting-like that your knitting friends might have to really inspect to make sure this was done with a hook. These toasty but fingers-free (so you can crochet with them on!) mittens are a dream to work because there are just two main stitches, and they are repeated throughout. Those bobble frills at the edges are worked at the same time as the rows, which really helps you keep track of where you are (each bobble marks two rows), and the only finishing needed is a seam up the side.

SKILL LEVEL
Beginner

FINISHED SIZE
- 8 in. by 8 in. laid flat as a square before sewing side seam. One size fits all (adults), with notes for adjustment in pattern.

YARN
- 1 skein Bernat® Softee® Baby, 100% acrylic (5 oz./140 g, 362 yd./331 m) in #16603030201 Aqua, Light (CYCA 3) weight

TOOLS
- U.S. size E hook (3.5 mm)
- Tapestry needle

GAUGE
- 20 sc = 4 in.

DIRECTION FOR WRIST WARMERS
With E hook, ch 39, turn.

Row 1: Sc 38 (38 sts), ch 2, turn.

Row 2: Sc 38 in back loop (BL) only of each sc in previous row. Place marker (PM) in BL of last sc (#38) made, in this row ch 3, work 5 dc into that same st in previous row that last sc was made into. Turn work.

Row 3: Join last st of previous row to BL (now a front loop, since work is turned) marked with marker, using sl st. This forms the bobble at the top of the rows. Remove marker. Hdc into BL of same st you just worked into. Hdc across row in each BL only for 37 more sts (38 sts), ch 2, turn.

Row 4: Hdc across row in BL only. PM into BL of last hdc (#38) made, ch 3, work 5 hdc into that same st in previous row that last hdc was made into. Turn work.

Row 5: Remove marker. Sc in BL only of each hdc in previous row (38 sts), ch 2, turn.

Row 6: Same as Row 2 (38 sts).

Rows 7–32: Same as Row 3 (38 sts).
By now you can see the pattern. We are doing a ribbing consisting of 2 rows of BL sc sts, ended with a bobble, followed by a ribbing consisting of 2 rows of BL hdc sts, followed by a bobble. Continue this pattern until Row 32, which you will know because you have reached the 16th bobble. Sl st to finish on next row as with any bobble. Do not break off yet.

FINISHING

You now have a big square of crocheted ribbing with bobbles along one edge of it. The WS is the side where you can see the fold-over rows at the bottom of the bobbles. With RS together, fold in half with bobbles along top edge, and pin along seam, leaving an opening at the area between 1½ in. and 3 in. from the straight bottom edge opposite the one with the bobbles (that's where your thumb pokes out). With pins still on outside, try on the wrist warmer to check if the thumb placement is okay. If you find the wrist warmer is too loose, frog a couple rows and repeat this process of pinning and trying on. If it is too tight, add another couple rows and bobble, following pattern. Unpin, weave in ends, and use length of yarn to sew along edge just as you pinned previously, on WS with RS together, leaving same opening and avoiding sewing along edges of bobble. Weave in ends of sewing yarn. Flip to RS so stitching is on inside. Now go wear 'em and be cozy!

Here's an Idea!

You can also make these with the bobbles around the hand edge, if you prefer that. Just move the thumb opening to the opposite end of the tube when you sew the edges.

All Choked Up

This winningly pretty project has two variations: one for you and one to give to a lucky friend, perhaps. But when you try either design, you'll likely find yourself inventing more ideas for embellishing the basic choker shape. The beauty of it: While the choker uses only a few different crochet stitches, it affords you practice with several important techniques, such as crocheting around the edge for a sharper finish, working (very briefly) in the round, and shaping the easiest leaves. It's a quick project for those who aren't wild about delayed gratification and a charming way to use up small amounts of yarn left over from other projects. Neither gauge nor exact yarn matches are crucial for these chokers, so loosen up and have fun.

SKILL LEVEL
Beginner

FINISHED SIZE
- Body of basic choker shape: 13 in. long, excluding strings and loop; 1¼ in. wide

YARN FOR FLOWER VERSION
- **Body of choker:** Small amount of 1 skein Loops & Threads® Impeccable™, 100% acrylic (4.5 oz./128 g, 268 yd./245 m) in #01310 Amethyst or other non-scratchy purple yarn (any fiber content) in Medium (CYCA 4) weight
- **Flower petals:** Small amount of 1 skein Lion Brand® Yarn Martha Stewart Crafts™ Extra Soft Wool Blend, 65% acrylic, 35% wool (3.5 oz./100 g, 165 yd./150 m) in #500 Bakery Box White or other white yarn (any fiber content) in Medium (CYCA 4) weight

- **Flower center (outer):** Small amount of 1 skein Lion Brand Yarn Martha Stewart Crafts Extra Soft Wool Blend, 65% acrylic, 35% wool (3.5 oz./100 g, 165 yd./150 m) in #506 Igloo or other pale blue yarn (any fiber content) in Medium (CYCA 4) weight
- **Flower center (inner):** Small amount of 1 skein Lion Brand Yarn Martha Stewart Crafts Extra Soft Wool Blend, 65% acrylic, 35% wool (3.5 oz./100 g, 165 yd./150 m) in #557 Lemon Chiffon or other pale yellow yarn (any fiber content) in Medium (CYCA 4) weight
- **Leaves and stem:** Small amount of 1 skein Red Heart® Soft®, 100% acrylic (5 oz./141 g, 204 yd./187 m) in #4420 Guacamole or other green yarn (any fiber content) in Medium (CYCA 4) weight

YARN FOR BUTTON VERSION

- **Body of choker:** Small amount of 1 skein Caron® Simply Soft®, 100% acrylic (6 oz./170 g, 315 yd./288 m) in #H970039727 Black or other non-scratchy black yarn (any fiber content) in Medium (CYCA 4) weight
- **Circles around button:** Small amount of 1 skein Red Heart Soft Touch, 100% acrylic (5 oz./141 g, 290 yd./266 m) in #4615 Hot Pink or other hot pink yarn (any fiber content) in Medium (CYCA 4) weight

NOTIONS

- **For button version:** 3¾-in. buttons in white, any style (I used antique ones I had on hand)

TOOLS

- U.S. size E hook (3.5 mm)
- Tapestry needle (if doing button version, make sure your needle can fit through holes in button)

GAUGE

- For both versions: 18 sc = 4 in.

DIRECTIONS FOR BODY OF CHOKER

With E hook and purple (flower version) or black (button version), ch 5. Turn.

Row 1: Sc in 2nd ch from hook, sc in remaining 3 ch, for 4 sc in row (4 sc). Ch 1, turn.

Rows 2–51: Sc 4, ch 1, turn. Your piece should measure 13 in., more or less.

Edging (see p. 98): Work additional 2 sc in last st of Row 51 to turn corner, then sc in each open space at edge of work all the way down the side of the choker. The spaces you dip your

hook into are the holes after the 1st st in each vertical row. When you reach the next corner sc 3 in corner st. Sc 1 after you turn corner, ch 80 to make loop that will become the 2 ties of the choker, sk sc at center of row, sc 1 to join loop to row again, sc 3 in corner. You have now turned the corner of the bottom edge. Sc up final long edge of choker as with opposite side. Sc 3 in corner, ch 4, and sl st to final corner (starting point for edge). Turn. Sc 5 around loop formed by attached ch-4 to form choker's loop. Sl st to corner st opposite to starting point for edging. Break off. Use tapestry needle to weave in both tails. Cut 80-ch loop in half at point where it turns. Fasten cut ends with knots.

FLOWER CHOKER DECORATIONS

White Petal Part of Flower
With white, ch 3. Join with sl st to form loop.

Row 1: Work 7 sc into loop (around loop). Join with sl st (7 sc).

Row 2: Ch 5, sl st into same st to join 1st petal to body of flower, sl st in next sc on loop, ch 5, sl st into same st. Rep around loop until 7 petals are formed, 1 in each sc. Sl st to fasten off. Break off. Use tapestry needle to weave in tails.

Center of Flower
Using blue yarn, ch 3. Join with sl st to form loop.

Row 1: Work 6 sc into loop (around loop). Join with sl st (6 sc). Break off. Use tapestry needle to weave in tails.

Edging of Choker

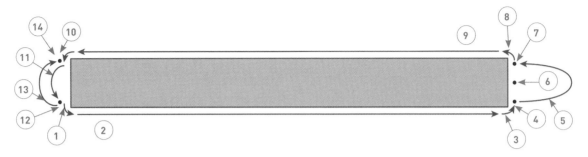

1. At the end of Row 51, place 2 additional sc in corner for 3 sc in that corner st.
2. Turn corner and sc down side of choker.
3. At last st of row/corner, sc 3 to turn corner.
4. Sc.
5. Ch 80 to form ch loop that will make ties.
6. Sk 1 sc.
7. Sc to next sc to join ch loop to choker.
8. Sc 3 in corner.
9. Sc down side as with opposite side.
10. Sc 3 in corner.
11. Ch 4.
12. Sl st to starting point corner.
13. Turn and sc 5 around loops formed by ch-4.
14. Sl st, break off.

Leaves (Make 2)
Using green, ch 7. Turn.

Row 1: In 2nd ch from hook, sl st. Sc in next st, then hdc, 2 dc, tr. Sc into the same ch you made the tr into, creating a rounded edge for the leaf. Break off. Weave in 1 tail and leave other for sewing onto choker.

Stem
Using green, ch 22. Leave long tails on both sides.

FINISHING
On RS of choker (side with chains of edging facing you), find midpoint of body of choker by folding in half. Pin one end of stem there and sew it, ch side up, using 1 tail end, at that center point and then down other half of choker to approximate what you see in the photo. Place each sewing st in center of ch st so sts don't show. Sew leaves to center point, weaving in ends at back of choker (no knots, please—this part goes against your neck). Thread tapestry needle with yellow yarn and knot end of yarn. Place blue center of flower on white petals and secure it there with a French knot. (To make French knot: Pull thread up through center of petals and blue center of flower, place tip of needle down near where stitch came up, wrap yellow yarn emerging from center of flower around needle 5 times, then poke needle down through center of flower in a slightly different spot.) Flatten knot with your fingers. Now use white yarn emerging from back of flower to sew flower onto choker at end of stem, slightly to the right of the leaves. Weave in ends of yellow and white yarn on WS of choker.

BUTTON CHOKER DECORATIONS

Pink Circles Beneath Buttons (Make 3)
Using pink, ch 3, sl st to 1st ch to form loop.

Row 1: Work 8 sc into loop (around loop), join with sl st (8 sc).

Row 2: *Work 2 sc into 1st sc, 1 sc into next sc, rep from * around loop (12 sc). Join with sl st. Break off. Using tapestry needle, weave in edge end of yarn, but leave center tail. Work carefully to keep circle as round as possible.

FINISHING

Thread needle with tail end of yarn at center back of each pink circle. Place button on top of pink circle and bring needle up through one buttonhole and down through another (if button has 4 holes, modify for that, stitching an X or 2 lines, whatever you like). With yarn coming from back of button now secured to circle, sew circles onto choker. Place one at center of choker and the others about 1½ in. away from it on either side. I found it useful to sew these to choker not through the buttonholes (which were pretty full of yarn) but in a circle of stitches around the edge of the button, on the surface of the pink circle. Keep circles as circular as possible. Weave in ends at back of choker without making knots.

Times Square Bag

Sheer need inspired this pattern. I wanted a small cross-body bag scarcely big enough to tote my phone, license, credit card, and sundry bucks as I trekked the heck out of NYC. Well . . . here it is, and I'm proud to report it rocks the house. It's light, handy, and secure, and I felt hip even in shops where my dress was definitely so last year. A few days later, I wore the black and white version to a formal wedding. You can shimmy with it on your dancing bod, and nobody will think you're that weird lady who can't let go of her handbag, even if you kind of are. The Times Square Bag makes use of the fun-to-hook shell pattern familiar from crocheted blankets. Those shellies give the bag enough texture to look woven, not crocheted. When worked in alternating colors, you get houndstooth, almost. Talk about checking your bags.

SKILL LEVEL
Beginner, but a little on the intermediate side at a few points explained fully

FINISHED SIZE
- Approx 5½ in. tall by 2¾ in. wide, not including strap. Notes for size adjustment are included in pattern.

YARN FOR GREEN VERSION
- 1 skein (you won't use it all) Red Heart Soft, 100% acrylic yarn (5 oz./141 g, 204 yd./ 187 m) in #4420 Guacamole or other non-scratchy green yarn (any fiber content) in Medium (CYCA 4) weight

YARN FOR BLUE VERSION
- 1 skein (again, you won't use it all) Lion Brand Yarn Martha Stewart Crafts Extra Soft Wool Blend, 65% acrylic, 35% wool (3.5 oz./100 g, 165 yd./150 m) in #506 Igloo or other non-scratchy pale blue yarn (any fiber content) in Medium (CYCA 4) weight

YARN FOR BLUE AND GREEN VERSION
- Smaller amounts of both of the above yarns

YARN FOR BLACK AND WHITE VERSION
- 1 skein (or, rather, part of it) Caron Simply Soft, 100% acrylic (6 oz./170 g, 315 yd./288 m) in #H970039727 Black or other non-scratchy black yarn in Medium (CYCA 4) weight

- 1 skein (you'll use way less) Lion Brand Yarn Martha Stewart Crafts Extra Soft Wool Blend, 65% acrylic, 35% wool (3.5 oz./ 100 g, 165 yd./150 m) in #500 Bakery Box White #500 or other non-scratchy white yarn (any fiber content) in Medium (CYCA 4) weight

TOOLS
- U.S. size E hook (3.5 mm)
- Tapestry needle

GAUGE
- 20 sc = 4 in.

DIRECTIONS FOR SOLID COLOR FRONT AND BACK PANEL

Front Panel
With blue or green and E hook, ch 14.

Row 1: Sc in 2nd ch from hook, sk the next 2 ch, dc 5 into next ch (this is the shell), sk 2 ch, sc into next ch, sk 2 ch again, dc 5 into next ch for the 2nd shell, sk the next 2 ch (see the pattern developing here?), sc into final st in row, turn.

Here is your chance to check whether your bag front will accommodate whatever you want to put into it. I held this row up to the base of my phone, and it was just wide enough to span the phone's bottom edge with a tiny bit of overlap on the sides. If your 1st row is not long enough to span the bottom horizontal edge of your phone, frog the whole project up to this point (1st row and chain row) and make a chain instead that is any multiple of 6 sts plus 2. Then repeat the pattern of the 1st row into that number of chains, ending with the sc in the final st in the row, and see how you like that width. Too big is okay, but too small, and you'll have to frog again or try it with a bigger hook.

Row 2: Ch 3, which forms your turning ch, dc 2 into sc at base of turning ch (1st st in row), sk 2 sc and then sc in next sc (3rd dc of previous row's shell), sk the next 2 dc, then dc 5 into next sc (which is between shells). Continue making an sc in 3rd dc of next shell top, then 5 dc into next sc, all the way across the row until you get to the end, where you dc 3 into final st in row. For the standard size of this pattern, this 2nd row is only 1 shell st in the middle of the row, with 2 3-dc half-shells at each end. Turn.

Row 3: Ch 1, sc in 1st dc of previous row, sk 2, work 5 dc into next sc in previous row. You are repeating Row 1 here, pretty much, except for the ch-1 that begins it.

Rows 4–14: Repeat Rows 2 and 3. Is your front panel tall enough after Row 14 to cover the entire front face of your phone? If yes, you're done with this panel; break off yarn. If no, add more rows.

Back Panel
Work exactly as for front panel, with same width of rows, but this time add extra rows of shells at the top so that the back panel can fold over the front in a nice flap. For the 14-row height of an iPhone® cover, I worked a back panel of 21 rows of shell sts. But again, eyeball it, and drape that back flap along the back of the phone and fold it over to approximate a flap. You may want the flap longer (in which case, keep adding rows) or smaller. You can also make a bag with even front and back panels, if you don't like or need the flap.

To form the latch that will go around the button, after you reach the end of your last row of shell sts on the back panel, turn, sc 4, ch 9 (to make the loop of the latch), then sc 4 more across row. Break off yarn and weave in end.

DIRECTIONS FOR TWO-COLOR FRONT AND BACK PANELS

Work just as for one-color versions, but alternate colors each row of shells. This will leave you with a lot of tails to weave in at the ends of the rows. Oh well. It's worth it!

If you are wondering which side of the shell pattern is the front and which is the back, guess what: You get to decide. Just pick the one you like better and have that face out on the bag. For me it was a tough call.

OPTIONAL INNER POCKET

I wanted to include a pocket inside the bag where my credit card/ID/cash could sit, so they wouldn't come flying out every time I extracted the phone. To make this inner pocket, grab your credit card or ID, then work enough chs to span the length of it one way (doesn't matter which). Work the 1st row and see if that still covers the credit card. If not, adjust length of ch. Then work additional rows of sc until crocheted piece is almost exactly the size of your credit card. For me, this worked out to be 10 sc sts across,

with 20 rows of them. Sew the inner pocket along three edges, leaving the top edge open, to the inside of the back panel.

STRAP

Using the no-foundation-chain double-crochet method described on p. 50 and whatever color yarn you want for the strap, work 198 dc. Make sure to leave about an 8-in. tail at the beginning of your work. This will give you a ½-in. strap, as shown in the photo. To check to see whether this strap is the length you desire, loop it across your body in a circle, like the strap of any cross-body bag. Remember that this strap encircles the bottom of the front and back panels, rather than hanging from just the top. That subtracts some from its length. If you want more length, crochet extra rows. If less, obviously, pull some out.

As the strap forms the sides (depth) of this bag, you may want to double that ½ in. if you have more things you want to fit into the bag. In that case, work an additional dc row on top of the row of 198, for a 1-in. strap.

Size Wise

While this design fits most smartphones (with non-bulky protective cases on them), the pattern includes instructions for customizing if your phone is bigger—or, say, if you want to work this for a passport carrier. There's also a way to check whether you are on track, sizing-wise, in the early stages of the project. Because it works up quickly and is an easily memorized pattern, this makes a sweet travel project and gift. You just have to play detective ahead of time and find out what size phone you're making it for.

BUTTON

This is an easy, squishy button worked in rounds. Feel free to substitute a regular button if you prefer.

Using whatever color you like, ch 2.

Round 1: Sc 8 into 2nd ch from hook for round of 8 sts.

Round 2: Work 2 sc into each sc in previous round (16 sts).

Round 3: Sc2tog all the way around to decrease (8 sts).

Round 4: Sc2tog all the way around again (4 sts). Leave a long tail when breaking off yarn. Flatten into button shape. Trim starting tail and poke into center of button to hide. Save remaining tail for sewing the button onto the front of the bag.

FINISHING

Weave in any tails on all pieces except the tail at one edge of the strap, and the end tail of the button.

Use the strap yarn tail end to sew the strap into a loop, being careful not to let it get twisted. Pin front panel to strap, centering strap seam at bottom edge of front panel. The front panel is attached to the bottom part of this big circle of strap along the sides and bottom of the front panel, with the top free. Because the width of the strap becomes the sides of the bag, sew only one lengthwise edge of the strap to the edge of the front panel (as the other long edge of the strap will be sewn to the edge of the back panel), as shown above.

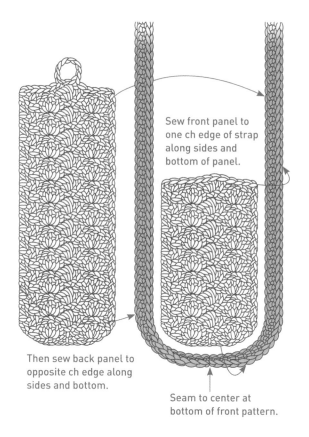

Sew front panel to one ch edge of strap along sides and bottom of panel.

Then sew back panel to opposite ch edge along sides and bottom.

Seam to center at bottom of front pattern.

Then sew the back panel to the same areas of the strap, leaving the top free, in the same manner. A few pins will help you keep it where you want it while you sew.

Using the button's tail end, sew the button to the front panel in center of 7th row of shells from bottom, fastening securely at center point and leaving edges of button free. Weave in remaining tail, giving it a few extra weaves for safekeeping.

Best-Dressed Plant

If a plant is going to hang, why not hang it in the plant equivalent of a beautiful crocheted sweater? This pattern is worked in the round, following a predictable sequence (so you probably won't have to refer to the pattern after a certain point). Many admirers might mistake the finished product for macramé, but it's so much more elegant and vastly less itchy and awkward to work. No tying anything to the leg of a chair, 1970s-style: just a hook and some yarn, this pattern, your willing lap. And, eventually, a very happy plant. Once you're familiar with the pattern, try it with a larger hook and a weightier yarn, or a smaller hook and thread-like yarn. It'll look like you've created different plant-holder designs just because of the scale.

SKILL LEVEL
Beginner

FINISHED SIZE
- About 25 in. from base to top of hook when unstretched. Fits a variety of flowerpots, with diameters of up to 7 in. It's super-easy to make the straps longer (add more chains to each strap), and if you want the top diameter wider, follow the sequence of the pattern for additional rows.

YARN
- 1 skein Lion Brand Yarn Cotton-Ease® 50% cotton/50% acrylic (3.5 oz./100 g (207 yd./188 m) in #099 Almond, Medium (CYCA 4) weight

TOOLS
- U.S. size E hook (3.5 mm)
- Tapestry needle

GAUGE
- 18 sc = 4 in.

DIRECTIONS FOR BASKET

With E hook, ch 12 and join with sl st to form a ring.

Round 1: Dip hook into center of ring and work an sc st around it, then sc 16 more in this way, enclosing the ring in your sts and joining at end with a sl st (17 sts covering ring). If you like, lay tail across this ring as you work, enclosing it in sts so you don't have to weave it in later.

Round 2: Ch 3, [2 tr, dc] into the sl st that ended round 1, at the base of the ch-3 you just worked (this forms your first cluster). *Ch 2, sk 2, work [dc, 2 tr, dc] into next st (this forms second cluster). Repeat from * around round so there are 6 clusters in round. Ch 2 and join with sl st to the top of the first ch 3 in this round. Sl st across tops of next two sts (first two sts of first cluster) to reach center of that first cluster of previous round.

Round 3: Ch 3, [2 tr, dc] into the center of the first cluster between the 2 trs. *Ch 1, dc into center of next ch sp between clusters, ch 1, work [dc, 2 tr, dc] into center of next cluster. Repeat from * for rest of round, ending with a dc worked into the center of the final ch sp. Ch 1, sl st to join to top of ch-3 at beginning of round. Sl st 2 across next 2 sts to reach center of first cluster of previous round.

Round 4: Ch 3, [2 tr, dc] into the center of the first cluster between the 2 trs. *Ch 4, work [dc, 2 tr, dc] into center of next cluster. Repeat from * for remainder of round, ending with ch 4. Sl st to top of ch-3 at beginning of round. Sl st across next 2 sts to reach center of first cluster of previous round.

Round 5: Ch 3, [2 tr, dc] into the center of the first cluster between the 2 trs. *Ch 2, dc into center of next ch sp between clusters, ch 2, work [dc, 2 tr, dc] into center of next cluster. Repeat from * for rest of round, ending with

a dc worked into the center of the final ch sp. Ch 2 and sl st to join to top of ch-3 at beginning of round. Sl st 2 across next 2 sts to reach center of first cluster of previous round.

Round 6: Ch 3, [2 tr, dc] into the center of the first cluster between the 2 trs. *Ch 6, work [dc, 2 tr, dc] into center of next cluster as in previous rows. Repeat from * for remainder of round, ending with ch 6. Sl st to top of ch-3 at beginning of round. Sl st across next 2 sts to reach center of first cluster of previous round.

Round 7: Ch 3, [2 tr, dc] into the center of the first cluster between the 2 trs. *Ch 3, dc into center of next ch sp between clusters, ch 2, work [dc, 2 tr, dc] into center of next cluster. Repeat from * for rest of round, ending with a dc worked into the center of the final ch sp. Ch 3 and sl st to join to top of ch-3 at beginning of round. Sl st 2 across next 2 sts to reach center of first cluster of previous round.

Round 8: Ch 3, [2 tr, dc] into the center of the first cluster between the 2 trs. *Ch 8, work [dc, 2 tr, dc] into center of next cluster as in previous rows. Repeat from * for remainder of round, ending with ch 8. Sl st to top of ch-3 at beginning of round. Sl st across next 2 sts to reach center of first cluster of previous round.

Round 9: Ch 3, [2 tr, dc] into the center of the first cluster between the 2 trs. *Ch 4, dc into center of next ch sp between clusters, ch 2, work [dc, 2 tr, dc] into center of next cluster. Repeat from * for rest of round, ending with a dc worked into the center of the final ch sp. Ch 4 and sl st to join to top of ch-3 at beginning of round. Sl st 2 across next 2 sts to reach center of first cluster of previous round.

Round 10: Ch 3, [2 tr, dc] into the center of the first cluster between the 2 trs. *Ch 10, work [dc, 2 tr, dc] into center of next cluster as in previous rows. Repeat from * for remainder of

Easy Strappings

Mark every other cluster, where the straps go.

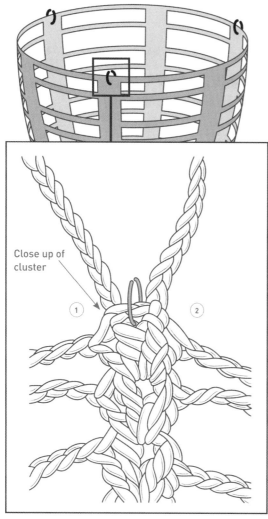

Close up of cluster

View from outside of basket. First chain of strap attaches to each cluster at ①. Then sl st to ② to ch 80 for second chain of strap.

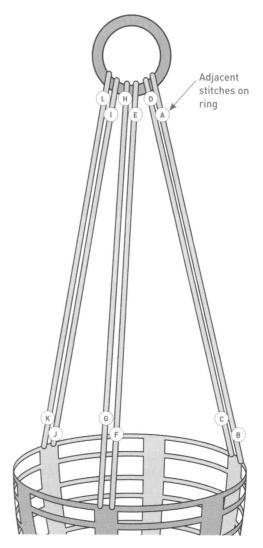

Adjacent stitches on ring

From point ⒶⒶ, ch 80 and attach at Ⓑ. Sl st to Ⓒ, ch 80 and attach at Ⓓ. Sl st to Ⓔ, ch 80 and attach at Ⓕ. Sl st to Ⓖ, ch 80 and attach at Ⓗ. Sl st to Ⓘ, ch 80 and attach at Ⓙ. Sl st to Ⓚ, ch 80 and attach at Ⓛ.

round, ending with ch 10. Sl st to top of ch-3 at beginning of round. Sl st across next 2 sts to reach center of first cluster of previous round.

Round 11: Ch 3, [2 tr, dc] into the center of the first cluster between the 2 trs. *Ch 5, dc into center of next ch sp between clusters, ch 2, work [dc, 2 tr, dc] into center of next cluster. Repeat from * for rest of round, ending with a dc worked into the center of the final ch sp. Ch 5 and sl st to join to top of ch-3 at beginning of round. Sl st 2 across next 2 sts to reach center of first cluster of previous round.

TO FORM RING AT TOP AND TWO-STRAND STRAPS

These are formed and assembled at kind of the same time. Use stitch markers (of some kind) to mark every other cluster in the top row of the basket portion you just finished (there will be 3 clusters marked). These are where your straps will attach.

First Strap

With same hook and yarn, ch 20. Sl st to form ring. Dip hook into center of ring and work an sc st around it, then sc 32 more in this way, enclosing the ring in your sts. Ch 33 into ring to cover it. Sl st to form ring, enclosing tail in ring if you prefer. Then ch 80 (this will be a strap). To help you keep track of the 80, place a marker every 20 sts. *Use a sl st to attach the end of 80th ch to a marked cluster between a dc and tr as shown in the close-up illustration. Sl st 2 to reach other side of this cluster, then ch 80 to make 2nd strand in this strap. Attach to ring with sl st beside the st where the first ch originated (see the illustration). Sl st 1 to reach st in ring to the right of this one. Here is where you will begin your next strap.

Second Strap

Ch 80, placing markers every 20 sts if that helps you keep track. Follow pattern for 1st strap from *, attaching this time to the 2nd cluster you have marked with a marker.

Third Strap

Work the same as the previous two, but attach to the 3rd cluster you have marked. Break off yarn, remove any markers, and weave in any remaining ends.

Mind Games

Should you find yourself without pencil or paper, working on a project in the round, how do you keep track of which round you're on? Some do it with markers, but another method is purely mental: just picture the number of the round—say, 5—clearly in front of you. Give it some detail: What color is this 5 you're picturing, and how big? Then silently chant "five, five, five, five" as you make your way around the round. Next row, conjure up your 6, very different in color or size, and picture that. Feels a little out-there at first, but it works and becomes much easier over time. Greeting each new round number with a feeling of celebration (Yay, 7!) helps, too.

Addictive Granny Square Mug Blankies

While teaching myself how to do a granny square, I uncovered Granny's little secret: These squares are killer fun! They're especially fun if you work them the way I do here, concealing the ends of new colors as you go. Each square completed gives the crocheter a burst of "Wow-it's-so-cute!" dopamine, and before you know it, you're fully addicted and need to make more *now*. No wonder there are so many afghans out there! Unfortunately, my home décor does not mesh with traditional granny squares well, nor do I have time at the moment to make a blanket. How to indulge in granny square glee without giving the world another couch-draper? These babies! Which are so adorable I can't stop staring at them on my counter. Someone come over for cocoa, fast, because not only are these mug cozies sweet, pleasing to touch, and functional (insulation = hotter beverage), they also transform mismatched mugs into a set. And like the Times Square Bag, they are ideal quick-project gifts.

Another thing Granny was hip to: You don't have to follow any particular color pattern with these. I used tones that reminded me of blue and white china, sometimes working two matching squares with a non-matching one between them, sometimes winging it from round to round with all three squares. One of my colors was variegated, which added some welcome surprise to the process. I am serious about the dopamine, by the way. Not even joking. Consider yourself warned.

SKILL LEVEL
Beginner

FINISHED SIZE
- Approx 9¾ in. wide by 3 in. tall

YARN
- The beautiful thing about granny squares is that you can use scraps from your bag. But I wanted these to look as cozy as possible, so I sprang for a yarn that was part wool, which will also insulate drinks better. The yarns I chose were all Bernat Sheep(ish)™ 70% acrylic/30% wool (3 oz./85 g, 167 yd./153 m) in Medium (CYCA 4) weight, but feel free to substitute whatever you like as long as the gauge works for your mug. You can always work one square, measure

it, and multiply its length by 3 to see if it makes a good wrap for whatever mug you're wanting to snuggle. Here are my colors of Sheep(ish):
    #00015 Robin Egg(ish) (light blue)
    #00014 Turquoise(ish) (turquoise)
    #00004 White(ish) (off-white)
    #0004 Stripes Homme(ish) (variegated)

- **Note:** The method of enclosing and snipping ends in this pattern works just fine for a fuzzy, grippy yarn and a project like this. But for a real gonna-use-it-forever granny square blanket made from a smoother yarn, I'd opt for a securing method that's even more secure, like the method on p. 63, which you can also use here if you prefer. This way's just quicker.

TOOLS

- U.S. size G hook (4 mm)
- U.S. size E hook (3.5 mm)
- Tapestry needle

GAUGE

- 16 sc = 4 in.

DIRECTIONS FOR BASIC GRANNY SQUARE (MAKE 3)

With G hook and 1st (center) color, ch 4. Sl st to 4th ch from hook to form ring.

Round 1: Ch 3. While holding tail along edge of ring at back of ring (so you can enclose it in the base of all the sts in this round), dc 2 (forms 1st cluster), ch 2, dc 3 (forms 2nd cluster), ch 2, dc 3 (forms 3rd cluster), ch 2, dc 3 (forms 4th cluster), ch 2, and attach to top of 1st ch-3 (turning ch) in round with sl st, to form round. Sl st 3 sts across top of 1st cluster to arrive at corner. Clip yarn about 4 in. from last st, remove loop from hook and pull clipped end through center of loop. Clip tail you've enclosed at center of ring close to base sts.

Round 2: Make slipknot with new color (2nd color from center). Stick empty hook through ch-2 space immediately following where the tail of 1st color is, put sl st onto hook, pull up through that ch-2 space, ch 3. Grab tails (ends) of 1st color and 2nd color together with non-hook hand and lay them across that ch-2 space to enclose tails/ends in back of bases of next 5 sts. Dc 2 more to complete 1st cluster in corner (while enclosing tails/ends), ch 2, dc 3 (this group of 2 clusters with 2 ch between is your 1st corner cluster). Snip tails/ends close to base of sts at back of work. Ch 1, then dc 3, ch 2, dc 3 in next ch space of previous round (the 2nd corner). Ch 1, then do same dc 3, ch 2, dc 3 in next ch space (3rd corner). Ch 1, dc 3, ch 2, dc 3 in final corner. Ch 1, sl st to attach to 1st corner, sl st 2 more sts across top of 1st cluster to arrive in corner. Clip yarn about 4 in. from last st, remove hook, and pull cut end through loop that was on hook.

Round 3: Make slipknot with new color (3rd color from center). Attach to corner ch-2 as described in Round 2. Ch 3, dc 2 into ch-2 space of 1st corner, enclosing tails as in Round 2, ch 2, dc 3 to form 1st corner clusters. Snip enclosed tails close to base at back of work. *Ch 1, dc 3 into next ch-2 space of previous round. Ch 1, dc 3, ch 2, dc 3 into next ch space of previous round (to form 2nd corner cluster). Repeat from * 2 more times. Ch 1, dc 3 into next ch-2 of previous round, ch 1, sl st to attach to 1st cluster. Sl st 2 more to arrive in corner. Clip yarn about 4 in. from last st, remove hook, and pull cut end through loop that was on hook.

BUTTON

This is an easy, squishy button worked in rounds. Feel free to substitute a regular button if you prefer.

With E hook and whatever color you like, ch 2.

Round 1: Sc 8 into 2nd ch from hook for round of 8 sts.

Round 2: Work 2 sc into each sc in previous row (16 sts).

Round 3: Sc2tog all the way around to decrease (8 sts).

Round 4: Sc2tog all the way around again (4 sts). Leave a long tail when breaking off yarn. Flatten into button shape. Trim starting tail and poke into center of button to hide. Save remaining tail for sewing the button onto the mug blankie.

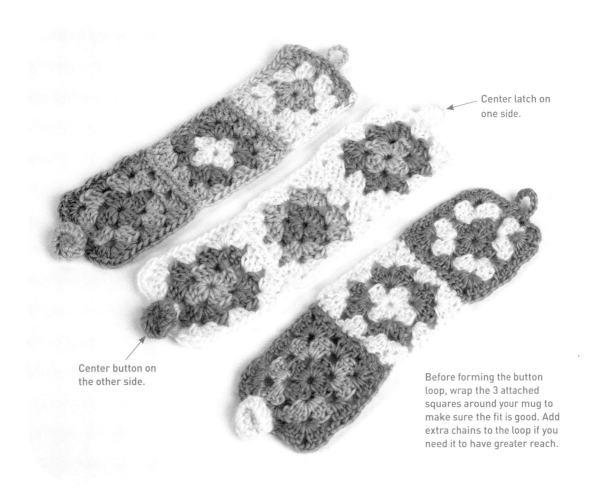

Center latch on one side.

Center button on the other side.

Before forming the button loop, wrap the 3 attached squares around your mug to make sure the fit is good. Add extra chains to the loop if you need it to have greater reach.

FINISHING

Weave in ends on 3 granny squares.

Lay 3 granny squares beside each other, in any order you'd like them to be attached. They're square, so you can orient them. If you want to pin them together, go ahead. Or you might be able to manage without pinning. Using mattress stitch (p. 68), sew the 1st to the 2nd where they meet, and then the 2nd to the 3rd, using whatever color matches the seam best. Weave in ends remaining after seam is sewn (if you use the slipknot method in the sidebar on p. 65, this will just be one end at top of seam).

Squish the button into the best button shape it can be, then use the tail of it to sew the button to the center of one of the short sides of the granny square strip.

On the opposite side of the 3-strip panel, form a loop that goes around the button as follows: At top of one edge of 3-dc cluster in center of side of panel, attach any color yarn by making slipknot, pulling through, then ch 8. Sl st to attach to other edge of 3-dc cluster in center of side panel. Snip yarn about 4 in. from sl st, remove hook, pull through loop. Then use tapestry needle to weave in ends of both sides of button loop.

Bubble-Wrap Scarf

The bobble stitch, or raspberry stitch, is just the niftiest dang thing, no? It creates rounded bumps, giving work a texture that begs to be touched, the same way bubble wrap does, but with so very much more sophistication. Here, the bobbles are scaled up, worked in thick yarn, with a hook fat as a marker. The work hums along quickly row by row, with really just four rows repeating, and the finished scarf seems to benefit, warmth-wise, from the depth of the stitches. If you wear it and a friend tries to poke at one of the bobbles, you'll know you've done your job right. This pattern can be worked in 2 styles, depending on the length you want. It can meet at the corners for a bottom edge that goes straight across, or it can fold over itself for a more diagonal closure. The difference is really only a few rows of crochet and a variation in closure.

SKILL LEVEL
Beginner

FINISHED SIZE
- Approx 6 in. wide by 20½ in. long for 1-button version, several inches longer for 3-button version, with easy instructions for lengthening if needed

YARN
- Lion Brand Yarn Wool-Ease® Thick & Quick®, 80% acrylic/20% wool (6 oz./170 g, 106 yd./97 m) in #640-105 Glacier, Super-Bulky (CYCA 6) weight

TOOLS
- U.S. size P hook (15.75 mm, in this case)
- Tapestry needle
- Button(s) of your choice (size shown: 1¾ in. diameter, but you can use any size)
- Thread or length of thinner yarn to sew on button(s)

GAUGE
- 8 sc = 4 in.

BOBBLE STITCH (BO)

The bobble stitch is like doing 5 dc stitches into a single stitch, but with the crucial difference that you don't quite finish those dc stitches. Then you gather them all into 1 stitch, thus creating *le perfect puff*. Confused? I was too. Here's the spelled-out way: *yo (as you would for a dc), insert hook into st, yo the hook, and pull that yarn through the st. You now have 3 loops on your hook. Yo and pull through the 2 loops closest to the tip of your hook, but not the 3rd. You have 2 loops on hook. At this point, yo, insert hook into same st you just worked that last partial dc into, yo the hook, and pull that yarn through the st. You now have 4 loops on your hook. Yo and pull again through the 2 loops on the hook closest to the tip of your hook, but not the 3rd and 4th. You now have 3 loops on your hook. Continue this process into the same st 2 more times until you have 5 loops on your hook. Your work should look like this:

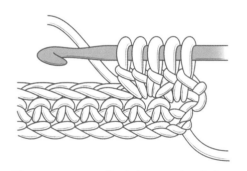

Then you yo one final time, and pull that yarn through all 5 loops to finish the st. You should be looking at something like this:

That's the whole story!

To Get Started
With P hook, ch 12.

Row 1: In 2nd ch from hook, sc. Sc across rest of row (11 sts). Ch 1, turn.

Row 2: Sc in 1st st, make bobble stitch (bo) in 2nd st, sc 3, bo, sc 3, bo, sc. Ch 1, turn. Admire them sweet bobbles!

Row 3: Sc all the way across the row (which is so boring, but think of it as your breather). Ch 1, turn.

Row 4: Sc 3, bo, sc 3, bo, sc 3. Ch 1, turn.

Row 5 (another cakewalk): Sc across row. Ch 1, turn.

Rows 6–38: Repeat Rows 2–5 until you have worked a total of 38 rows. Now try wrapping the scarf around your neck, consulting the photo for this finished pattern to see if yours is fitting you (or your likely recipient) the way you want it to. If you prefer it longer, add more rows. Just make sure you finish after one of the sc rows, so both ends look finished at the same point. Note that if working the 1-button variation, where the edges meet at the corner, you'll need less length than if working the 3-button variation, where the edges fold over. To test whether the 3-button version is long enough, fold it over your neck as shown and pin along the edge, then see if it slips over your head comfortably, because in this version the buttons are merely decorative and do not fasten or unfasten. See the illustrations on p. 118.

FINISHING

Break off yarn and weave in ends. If the eye of your usual tapestry needle is way too small to be threaded with this seriously thick yarn, split the strand into two, and weave each piece of it in separately.

Drape the scarf around your neck, a dress form, or some cooperative person's neck so you can see how it will come together. Here are the two shapes of the scarf:

One-Button Version

Sew button near top edge of one long side, centered between 1st row of bobbles and second, in a flat spot.

Form a loop as follows on the opposite edge of the scarf directly across from the button: Using the same yarn you used for the piece, make a slipknot. Then dip your hook into the place where you want one edge of the loop to be (mine is at the beginning of the 3rd row up from the edge on this side), hold the slipknot on the underside of this spot, slip it onto the knot, and pull through. Now ch 5 to form loop. Then dip hook back into scarf about 1 row up, and pull yarn through to attach.

Break off ends, and use your tapestry needle to weave them in. Fasten the loop around the button, and you're good to go.

Three-Button Variation

Once you are sure the length of your scarf will work when sewed along the edges as shown in illustration on p. 118, sew edges marked, then sew 3 buttons between the bobbles along the side between corner B and the center point of the scarf. No need to make loops for these buttons because they are merely decorative.

One-Button Version

This version sits a little lower on the neck, like a mini-cape.
Looks amazing under a jacket or sweater.

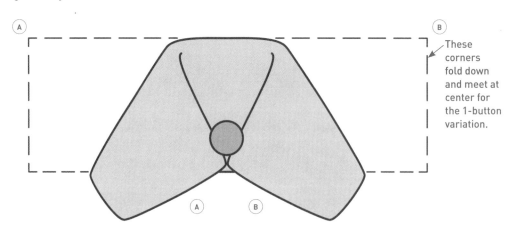

These corners fold down and meet at center for the 1-button variation.

Three-Button Version

This one folds over in a way that provides an extra layer of warmth. Great for friends in cold places.

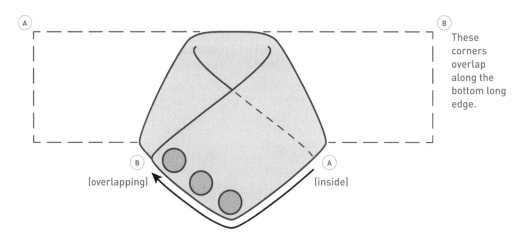

(overlapping)   (inside)

These corners overlap along the bottom long edge.

Sew along edges from (B) to (A) for the 3-button variation.

Cheat Sheet

For those (rare, we know!) moments when your brain goes blank and you can't remember how to do the basic crochet stitches, here's the lowdown.

Slip stitch (sl st): Starting with a row of chain stitches, insert your hook into the 2nd chain from the hook. Wrap the yarn over the hook (yo), and pull that yarn through both loops on the hook.

Single crochet (sc): Starting with a row of chain stitches, insert your hook into the 2nd chain from the hook. Wrap the yarn over the hook (yo), and pull that yarn through the chain you've stabbed the hook through. Yo again and pull that yarn through both loops on the hook.

Half-double crochet (hdc): Like single crochet, but you wrap the yarn over the hook (yo) before inserting the hook into the 3rd chain from the hook. Yo a 2nd time and pull that yarn through the stitch you've just stabbed into. Yo a 3rd time and pull through all 3 loops on the hook.

Double crochet (dc): Wrap the yarn over the hook (yo) before inserting the hook into the chain. Yo again and pull through the stabbed chain stitch. Yo a 3rd time and pull through the 2 loops on the hook closest to the tip of it. Yo a 4th time and pull through those last 2 loops on the hook. Double crochet rows start with a turning chain of 3 (or 2, if you prefer), so when starting the 1st row, you insert the hook into the 4th (or 3rd, if you prefer) chain from the hook.

Half-treble/half-triple crochet (htr): Yo twice and insert hook into 5th chain from hook (or 4th, if you prefer). Yo a 2nd time and pull through the stitch you've just stabbed through. Yo a 3rd time and pull that yarn through the 2 loops on the hook closest to the tip of the hook. Yo a 4th time and pull through the 3 remaining loops on the hook.

Treble/triple crochet (tr): Yo twice and insert hook into 5th chain from hook (or 4th, if you prefer). Yo a 2nd time and pull through the stitch you've just stabbed through. Yo a 3rd time and pull that yarn through the 2 loops closest to the tip of the hook. Yo a 4th time and pull through the 2 loops closest to the tip of the hook. Yo a 5th time and pull through the remaining 2 loops on the hook.

Decrease by working a single crochet into the next 2 stitches (sc2tog): You can also decrease in this way for taller stitches. The idea is to almost make 2 complete stitches, but then finish them with 1 stitch. So for single crochet, you would insert the hook into the next stitch, yo, and draw that yarn through the stabbed stitch. Then, instead of finishing off that single crochet stitch, insert your hook into the next stitch, yo, and draw that yarn through the stabbed stitch. There are now 3 loops on the hook. Yo one final time and draw that yarn through all 3 stitches. You've just made 1 stitch out of 2, so your row (or round) has gotten smaller. For less noticeable decreases for amigurumi, see p. 86.

Work around front of post/back of post: This sounds like instructions for a stripper, does it not? Nothing that exciting. Instead, it applies to working stitches not into the V-shaped thing at the top of the stitch, but around the post (tall part) of a tall stitch, like double crochet or higher. To work a double crochet around the front of the post of a double crochet, yo and stab your hook into your work just to the right of the post (tall part) of the double crochet stitch you're working around. Then poke the hook back up through your work on the other side of that double crochet stitch. Now yo again and complete the double crochet stitch. For working around the back of the stitch, it's the same thing, but instead you first poke the hook from the back of the work to the front, just to the right of the double crochet stitch you're working around, and then poke your hook from the front of your work to the back on the other side of that double crochet stitch, and then you complete the stitch. This is a right-handed instruction, of course, but the same idea applies for left-handers. Front of post means you stab into it from the front first, and back of post means poke through from the back first.

Meet Our Crochet Stars!

Wanna know more about the amazing craftsters who contributed to this book? You should, because they're awesome. Here's the scoop:

San Francisco-based artist **Twinkie Chan**, she of the colorful hair and imagination, is the author of *Twinkie Chan's Crochet Goodies for Fashion Foodies.* You really haven't understood the cuteness and humor of crochet until you've checked out Twinkie's work, which often features crocheted food. See her goods at www.twinkiechan.com or purchase them via www.etsy.com or www.yummyyouclothing.com, her own clothing and accessories line. Twinkie has been crocheting since she was 10 years old, when her BFF's grandmother taught her how.

Edie Eckman, pretty much the queen of crochet, has written so many beautiful crochet books, including *The Crochet Answer Book*, *Around the Corner Crochet Borders*, *Beyond the Square Crochet Motifs*, and *Christmas Crochet.* She used to own a yarn shop, and is just as adept at knitting as at crochet (she has many fine books on that topic, too). You can see her work at www.edieeckman.com or her teaching at www.craftsy.com. She also designs patterns, writes columns for magazines and other publications, and teaches nationally.

A designer/writer/blogger in Iowa, **Tamara Kelly** unleashed her website www.mooglyblog.com as a mommy blog (her daughter invented the word *moogly*), but soon she began using it to share crochet and knitting patterns, tutorials, and general helpful thoughts. It's gotta be one of the best fiber arts websites out there, and she has a winningly effective way of explaining things. Plus, her good attitude comes shining through, and the photos are so inspiring you'll have a hard time keeping your hands from a hook after viewing them. Also, look for her on YouTube, especially if you're in a jam about technique.

Sandra Paul's website Cherry Heart (sandra-cherryheart.blogspot.co.uk) is where you should immediately go if your soul ever feels starved for crafting beauty. A wizard at combining pretty colors, she creates breathtaking designs with a sweet and romantic and homespun flavor to them. Sandra lives in Bedfordshire, England, and quilts, sews, and knits in addition to her crochet work. Her crocheting, knitting, and sewing patterns are available at her website. She also has a Ravelry group: Cherry Heart's Cozy Corner.

Alicia Paulson, a former boutique owner and book editor, has been crafting her whole life— and the accumulated expertise shows. She is the author of *Stitched in Time: Memory-Keeping Projects to Sew and Share from the Creator of Posie Gets Cozy*, and *Embroidery Companion: Classic Designs for Modern Living.* Alicia has two swoon-inducing websites you can visit: www.aliciapaulson.com and www.posiegetscozy.com, her blog. Sample either and you'll see how smart her eye is, and the former sells not only patterns for her delicious designs, but also supplies and kits to help you make them.

Index